THE UNITED FREE CHURCH

THE
UNITED FREE CHURCH

AN HISTORICAL REVIEW
OF TWO HUNDRED AND TWENTY-FIVE YEARS

1681-1906

BY

Rev. ROBERT LOGAN
Late of the Free Church, Abington and Crawfordjohn

AUTHOR OF
"GENEALOGICAL CHART OF THE ROYAL FAMILY OF GREAT BRITAIN"
"MEMOIR OF JAMES WALKER, D D ," ETC

WIPF & STOCK · Eugene, Oregon

Wipf and Stock Publishers
199 W 8th Ave, Suite 3
Eugene, OR 97401

The United Free Church
An Historical Review of Two Hundred and Twenty Five Years,
1681-1906
By Logan, Robert
Softcover ISBN-13: 978-1-7252-9912-2
Hardcover ISBN-13: 978-1-7252-9913-9
eBook ISBN-13: 978-1-7252-9914-6
Publication date 2/1/2021
Previously published by MacNiven & Wallace, 1906

This edition is a scanned facsimile of the original edition
published in 1906.

Dedicated

TO THE
MEMBERS OF THE UNITED FREE CHURCH WHO BELONGED
TO HER OLDEST SECTION, THE REPRESENTATIVES
OF THE HILL MEN AND SOCIETY MEN
OF LANARKSHIRE, AYRSHIRE,
DUMFRIESSHIRE AND
GALLOWAY
BY THE AUTHOR

PREFACE

THE subject matter of what is contained in the following pages was delivered as a Lecture under the title of "The Component Parts of the United Free Church" to the Guild of St. Mary's, Moffat, in December 1904 Some explanation is perhaps due for its appearing in an extended form. That explanation is twofold

The United Free Church may be compared to a river composed of four streams—the Reformed Presbyterian, The Secession, The Relief, and the Free Church Each of the members of the Church may be supposed to have a fair acquaintance with the history of the section in which he or she was brought up. There is a lack of books containing the necessary information everyone ought to possess regarding the other sections. I have traced the story from the formation of the oldest section, which happens to be the smallest, thus endeavouring to dovetail each into those that precede, and to treat the Church as a unit. In doing so, I have stated my opinions freely. I need hardly say I am alone responsible for them. They have been adopted not rashly, but after due deliberation. The mode of treatment has not unnaturally been influenced by the judgment of the House of Lords, 1st August 1904. I have thus been led to deal perhaps too exclusively with the external, that is to say, the historical and legal aspects of the subject. I have not felt myself called upon to dwell on the question of property. I have not been able to direct attention at any length to the internal or spiritual aspect. Nor have I ventured to treat the interesting topic of the Hand of God in His dealings with the Scottish Church. This would form material for a volume of considerable size, and could be adequately dealt with only by one fully acquainted with the history of the Protestant Churches of England, Ireland, and the Continent.

The second explanation is a personal one. I voted with the Free Church minority on the Union question up till May 1900, and my name will be found adhibited to the Reasons of Dissent laid on the Table of successive Assemblies. I did this chiefly from a fear that the Testimony of the Church to the Headship of the Mediator over all things might be weakened. But I had no sympathy with the opposition to the Declaratory Act, the Church's relation to Historical Criticism, or the conduct of praise in the Worship of the Sanctuary. If I had joined the Free Church of 1900 and 1904, I would have had to leave her in the latter year on account of her acquiescence in the grounds on which the Judges of the House of Lords appear to have based their decision. The property is held by the successful litigant for adhering to a semi-illegal document, and, to say the least of it, a quasi-Erastian Revolution Settlement. Does not the present Free Church rest on the handiwork of man rather than on the principles contained in God's Word? I have not attempted to discuss the question of the State's relation to the Church and religion. The solution of this problem seems to lie under and behind King William's Settlement, in the Civil Power's realising her subordination to the Mediator King. How this can be done only the future can evolve.

I venture to direct attention to the Appendix. I am indebted to Dr. Hay Fleming for permission to publish the " Children's Bond," to the Rev. James Hunter, Lauriston, for the list of the Moderators of the Reformed Presbyterian Church, to the family of the late Rev. Dr. Small for the use of their father's lists of those of the Burgher, Anti-Burgher, Secession,

Contents

APPENDIX—

 I. The Children's Bond 205

 II. Tabular View of the Ministers of the Churches of Scotland, 1662 and 1843 208

 III. List of Moderators and Professors of the Reformed Presbyterian, Associate, Burgher, Anti-Burgher, United Secession, Associate Burghers, Original Secession, Relief, United Presbyterian, and Free Churches . 216

 IV. Table of Some of the Events in Scottish Ecclesiastical History 261

INDEX 267

THE UNITED FREE CHURCH.

CHAPTER I.

INTRODUCTORY: 1560, 1638, 1660, 1681.

ON the 18th of May 1843, before noon, the Lord High Commissioner of Queen Victoria to the General Assembly of the Church of Scotland, John, Second Marquis of Bute, the great-grandson of the Prime Minister of George III.'s early days, held his levée in the public gallery of Holyrood. He had been Commissioner in the previous year, appointed by Sir Robert Peel during his second ministry. The levée was largely attended, for many of those present intended that afternoon to leave the National Establishment and not to return to it. They were paying their last token of respect to the representative of the Sovereign. As the crowd advanced they seem to have pressed upon the portrait of William III., which fell from its place. Then a voice, that of William Howeson Crawford of Crawfordland, was heard exclaiming: "There goes the Revolution Settlement!" That Settlement had been altered when the Patronage Act was passed by the British Parliament in 1712. It was again altered in the Act of 1874, when the appointment of ministers was practically placed in the hands of the congregation. What other alterations it may yet undergo the future will reveal.

The Revolution Settlement divides the History of the Reformed Church of Scotland into two periods of unequal length, the one extending from 1560 to 1690, a period of one hundred and thirty years. The other continues to the present time, two hundred and sixteen years.

We have to deal with the second of these. But we must look for a little at the first. We will confine ourselves almost exclusively to those points which throw light on subsequent events. On

Introductory 3

the cover of the *Missionary Record* of the United Free Church will be seen several dates — 1560, 1638, 1733, 1761, 1843, 1847, 1876, 1900. To these dates, and a few others, we intend to refer: 1560 and 1638 belong to the earlier period.

In the year 1560, the Scottish Parliament adopted the Scottish Confession known as Knox's Confession, and abolished Popery, and the first General Assembly of the Presbyterian Church was held. The Reformation movement had then been in existence about thirty-eight years. It had been chiefly confined to the central counties and the West of Scotland. Although many were subjected to banishment, imprisonment, or confiscation of goods, only twenty or twenty-one persons suffered martyrdom. From 1513, when the fatal Battle of Flodden was fought, till the return of Queen Mary from France in 1561, the nation had not a strong civil government except from 1528 to 1542, when James V. held the power in his own hands. This weakened the power of those opposed to the new movement. Till the settlement of Knox in Edinburgh—1559—Scotland cannot be said to have had a reformer. Patrick Hamilton was a teacher, George Wishart a preacher. It is interesting, but perhaps fruitless, to speculate what would have been the complexion of Protestantism in our country if the lives of these two or those of James IV. and V. had been preserved. The Word of God, circulated, read, preached, was the Reformer of Scotland. The Act of 1560 regarding the Scots Confession, which was drawn up by the six Johns—Winram, Willock, Douglas, Spottiswoode, Row and Knox, was ratified by the Parliament of 1567, a few months after the infant king was crowned—the same Parliament that established the Church. What we have to note here is that there was a National Confession, not only before a National Church, but even before the first General Assembly was held. For seven years the Protestant Church was not connected with the State. The Creed came first, the Church second.

Introductory

The Church of the Reformation continued to 1638, when it became the Church of the Covenant. During these seventy-eight years, the period of a long lifetime, the nation was distracted by the constant conflict between Church and State, the former asserting her Spiritual Independence, the latter attempting to limit or encroach upon it. The conflict has been carried on till our day, and is likely to continue for an indefinite time. It has been at the root of nearly all our ecclesiastical divisions. The question as to what is the line of demarcation between the Civil and Ecclesiastical seems to have a special fascination for the Scottish mind. It would almost appear as if the Living Head of the Church had assigned to the nation the work of solving it. Andrew Melville set it before King James VI. at Falkland in 1596, forcibly and pithily in the well-known saying: "There is twa Kings and twa Kingdoms in Scotland. There is Christ Jesus the King, and His Kingdom the Kirk, whase subject King James the Saxt is, and of whase

Kingdom not a king, nor a lord, nor a heid, but a member!" Four years earlier, in 1592, Parliament passed the Act known as the Great Charter of the Church, ratifying its government. A few years later Episcopacy was introduced through the Royal influence, an Episcopacy of a more modified type than that of England. The removal of the Court to London after James's accession to the English throne influenced the future of the Church of Scotland. It is impossible to say what course her history might have taken if the Sovereign had continued to reside in Edinburgh. Charles I., a conscientious, if not bigoted, Episcopalian, was not satisfied with the cautious policy of his father. His zeal led to the attempt to introduce the Liturgy that erroneously bears the name of Archbishop Laud, to the riot in St. Giles's in 1637, associated with the name of Jenny Geddes, and, with other causes, to the signing of the National Covenant and the meeting of the Glasgow Assembly in 1638. That memorable Assembly, the greatest Scotland has ever seen, continued its sittings after the Marquis of Hamilton, the Royal Commissioner, had withdrawn, abolished Episcopacy with the approval of a large proportion of every class of the community, and asserted, as has never been done before or since, the independence of the Protestant Church.

We cannot now enter into the tangled web of the history of the Civil War. Suffice it to say, the entanglements of the period led to the first breach among the Presbyterians, that between the Resolutionists and Protesters. But it must be remembered that the fifth decade of the XVII century was the golden age of the Presbyterian Church, the era of free assemblies, and of religious revival in the south and west of the land. During these years there lived some of the ablest, most learned and godly ministers the Church has produced, the statesmanlike Henderson, the Moderator of 1638, 1641, 1643; Dickson, Gillespie, Baillie, Douglas, Rutherford, all, with perhaps the exception of the last, too little remembered.

Before we pass on, we must refer to the Westminster Assembly. It was called in 1643 by the English Parliament and thus had an Erastian origin which was perhaps unavoidable. It sanctioned the Solemn League and Covenant, a document intended to secure the uniformity of religion in England, Scotland and Ireland, and drew up its Confession and Catechisms for the three kingdoms. The Confession was adopted by the General Assembly held at Edinburgh in 1647, and approved by the Estates of Parliament two years later. It does not appear that anyone was asked to sign it, signatures having been required for the Covenant. The Scottish Confession seems to have been silently dropped. In 1647, unlike 1560, it was Church first, Creed second.

The next three dates we have to refer to are not on the cover of our *Record*. The first of these is 1660, the year of the Restoration of Charles II.

Introductory

In the first Parliament of that monarch were passed the Recissory Act, annulling the legislation of the preceding years since 1640, another, restoring the Bishops, and a third, requiring all ministers of parishes who had not obtained a presentation from a patron to do so. The effect of the last measure was that fully a third of the ministers demitted their charges in 1662. These were among the youngest and the best. Only one of the ministers of Edinburgh remained within the Established Church. He received the name of the "nest egg," and eventually died a Bishop. Only four ministers in the Synod of Galloway retained their parishes. The Presbytery of Paisley came out to a man. In those of Dumfries and Hamilton, only one adhered to the Establishment; and in that of Biggar, only two. Very few ministers in the northern counties adhered to the Covenanters. The ousted ministers were forbidden to meet in Presbytery. Several of them suffered persecution, though only one, the well-known Donald Cargil, of the Barony,

Glasgow, died the martyr's death. The other martyr ministers of the Covenant were all ordained subsequent to the Restoration.

We cannot linger over the well-known story of the twenty-eight years of the reigns of Charles II. and James VII. The Episcopacy of the Restoration was not identical with that of England. The machinery of Presbytery, except the General Assembly, was in operation. The worship of the Church was very similar to that of the period immediately preceding. The Established Church of the day can hardly be said to have had a Confession. The old Confession seems to have received some kind of recognition by the State. The Covenanters adhered to the Westminster. Their followers were found chiefly in the southern and western counties. They differed upon the question of accepting the indulgences offered to their ministers by the Government. The extreme section separated from those who accepted or even in the slightest degree approved of them. Their leaders were Cargil, the "Veteran of the Covenant," and Richard Cameron, the "Lion of the Covenant."

Richard Cameron is perhaps the most striking figure in the roll of the men of mark connected with the story of the Reformed Churches in Scotland. Born at Falkland, he, like several of them, both before and after him, was connected with the County of Fife. Like Alexander Henderson and James Guthrie, the first martyr of the Covenant, he was brought up under Episcopal influences. His career as a Covenanting preacher naturally divides itself into two portions—the one before, the other after his residence in Holland. The story of his ordination will not be soon forgotten. It took place in the old Scots Church, Rotterdam. When two of the officiating ministers, Brown of Wamphray and a Dutchman named Koelman, had removed their hands from his head, the remaining one, Robert M'Ward, formerly of Glasgow, allowed his to remain, saying, "Behold all ye beholders, here is the head of a faithful minister and servant of Jesus Christ, who shall lose the same for his Master's interests, and shall be set up before sun and moon in the public view of the world."

These words, ascribed by some to the prophetic spirit, proved true. Cameron returned to Scotland shortly after the rout at Bothwell Bridge. On the first anniversary of that event, about twenty men rode into a small Scots town with drawn swords and pistols. Two dismounted at the market-place. When they arrived at the Town Cross, the one gave out a Psalm and engaged in prayer. The other read the document now known as the First Sanquhar Declaration and affixed it to the cross of the burgh. After further devotional exercises, they, with their companions, departed. These men were Richard Cameron and his brother Michael. In the Declaration they disowned the authority of King Charles II. This Act was the precursor of the Revolution.

Exactly a month later, on Thursday, 22nd July, the Camerons fell at Airsmoss in conflict with Royal troops under the command of Bruce of Earlshall. Of Richard Cameron, it has been said he "lived praying and preaching, and died praying and fighting." Wherein lay the charm connected with this young man of little education and probably more scanty worldly wisdom, whose ordained ministry lasted little more than half a year and was confined to the South and West of Scotland? His career reminds us of that of John the Baptist. Their ministries were short and confined to small districts of country. Their deaths were bloody. The burden of their preaching was similar —repentance. There was a tenderer tone, as became the minister of the New Testament, in that of the later, of him whose favourite theme at Rotterdam was "Come unto Me all ye that labour and are heavy laden and I will give you rest," who addressed, at Hyndbottom, the parishioners of Auchinleck, Muirkirk, Douglas, and Crawfordjohn from the words, "Ye will not come unto Me that ye might have life," with such pathos that he and they fell into a "calm weeping."

Three days after the fight at Airsmoss, on the Lord's Day, 25th July 1680, Donald Cargil preached at Shotts a funeral sermon for his young comrade. He took for his text the words of David regarding Abner the son of Ner, "Know ye not that there is a prince and a great man fallen this day in Israel," 2 Samuel, iii. 38. May we not apply to Cameron the words of the king, "Died Abner as a fool dieth? Thy hands were not bound nor thy feet put into fetters, as a man falleth before wicked men so fellest thou." We picture the young man of thirty as fearless and resolute, single-minded and tender-hearted, trusting firmly in and fired with devoted love to the person of his Incarnate Lord. He has left a name that will be long remembered. That name he did not give to his followers, nor did they assume it. But it has been bestowed upon them by their fellow-countrymen.

Fully a year after his death, these followers, without a recognised minister,

Introductory

formed themselves into societies, and were called the Society Men. They held their first meeting at Loganhouse, Lesmahagow parish, on 17th December 1681. Their most recent historian states they were seven thousand in number, besides women, and these Societies he reckons about eighty. They met chiefly in Galloway, and in retired spots in that region where the Counties of Dumfries, Ayr, and Lanark touch each other. An interesting circumstance may here be mentioned. There is a Bond extant, similar in spirit to the National Covenant, drawn up by fifteen girls dwelling in the village of Pentland. One of them, whose name is affixed to the document, lived to ninety years of age, and died after George III. ascended the throne.

For nearly six years, 1683-88—from his twenty-second to his twenty-seventh year—James Renwick ministered to the Societies, bearing their burdens during the stormy period of the persecution. Born at Moniaive, in Dumfriesshire, on the 15th February 1662, a few months after the execution of Argyle and Guthrie, and in the same year that the Covenanting ministers renounced their connection with the Establishment, his life ran parallel with the period of the persecution. Witnessing the martyrdom of Cargil, he resolved to take up his work. He was ordained at Groningen in Holland, and on his return to his native land entered on his work. We cannot linger on the story of his wanderings and escapes. Suffice it to say he was in labours abundant, and in journeyings and perils oft. He had the care of all the churches. He travelled, he preached, he administered the sacraments, he carried on a large correspondence. Accompanied by two hundred men, he affixed the second Sanquhar Declaration to the cross of that town. When brought before the Privy Council, he admitted the charges brought against him of not owning the King's authority, not paying cess, and advising his followers to attend his services armed. Every effort was made to induce him to recant, but, like many martyrs in all ages and many

Introductory

lands, he remained firm. On the scaffold he professed his adherence to the Westminster Standards and the Covenant, and protested against Erastianism and "against all usurpations and encroachments made upon Christ's right, the Prince of the kings of the earth, Who alone must bear the glory of ruling in His own kingdom the Church." Among his last words were, "Now, Lord, I am ready. The bride, the Lamb's wife, has made herself ready." Thus died, on the 17th February 1688, aged twenty-six years and two days, the youthful, amiable, gentle, catholic-spirited James Renwick. This boy preacher and martyr of the Covenant, the first minister of the Societies, should stand along with Cameron, and perhaps Cargil, at the head of the long catalogue of the ministers of the United Free Church, as 1681, the date of their formation, is the first in our annals. For these Societies formed the stem from which the oldest section of our Church sprang.

CHAPTER II.

THE REVOLUTION SETTLEMENT, 1689-1690: THE REFORMED PRESBYTERIANS, 1690-1863.

WE now come to the third date we have already referred to as not marked on the cover of the United Free *Record*, that of the Revolution Settlement, 1690. What had been rebellion at Pentland, Drumclog, Bothwell Bridge, Sanquhar, and Airsmoss, was Revolution in 1688. The English and Scots, for nearly a century, had been contending for their civil and religious liberties, and now they obtained the victory. On the Settlement as a fair basis rose our new constitution. On it stands the constitution that has been and is still being reared. James VII. was declared in the Scots Claim of Right to have "forefaulted the right to the Crown." That was offered to and accepted by his daughter and son-in-law, the second Mary Stuart and William of Orange. The Revolution forms an epoch not merely in the history of Britain, but of the civilised world. It has been called "glorious," and politically it was so.

When we turn to the ecclesiastical side of it, the judgment must be less favourable. A Reformed Presbyterian called it truly "a great relief"; an intelligent countryman, doing "a right thing in a wrong way." It was, to say the least of it, quasi-Erastian. This was probably unavoidable owing to the complications of the times. The Bishops, and several of the incumbents of parishes, refused to take the oath to the new sovereigns. They thus excluded themselves, and therefore were excluded from the Settlement. But for this the Settlement might have been different. A modified Episcopacy might have been established as in Ireland with a strong Presbyterian church outside, or Presbyterianism with a strong Episcopacy outside. The northern counties seemed to have favoured the one, and the central and southern the other. Presbytery and Episcopacy now parted company. To the latter we do not intend again to refer.

The Parliament of 1690 repealed all laws in favour of Prelacy, declared the government of the Church to be vested in the ministers who had been ejected at the Restoration and those who had been, or would be, admitted by them. It ratified a Confession of Faith, revived the Act of 1592, the Charter of the Church, and appointed the General Assembly to meet. The Confession selected was not the Scots Confession of Knox, which had been associated, however slightly, with the Restoration period, but the English one prepared at Westminster. The Act of Parliament describes it as the "public and avowed Confession of this Church," which it had been for about fifteen years. Here we have, as at the Reformation, Creed first and Assembly second.

The history of the Westminster Con-

The Revolution Settlement

fession is interesting. Drawn out as a Confession for England, Scotland, and Ireland, it was only retained in the second of these, and yet has become the Confession of English-speaking Presbyterians throughout the world. Its merits are many. Its demerits are those of the age of its authors. Does its presence on the Scottish Statute book make the nation a religious and ecclesiastical community, in fact a Church? Another Act of the Parliament of 1690 abolished Patronage, placing the selection of the ministers in the hand of the Heritors and Elders of parishes. The Recissory Act of Charles II. was not repealed, and the Covenant was ignored.

On 16th October the General Assembly met for the first time for thirty-seven years. Its Moderator was Hew Kennedy, an old Protester, then minister of the Trinity College Church, Edinburgh, known as Father Kennedy, and nicknamed by his opponents, Bitter Beard. It consisted of one hundred and eighty members. It cannot be called representative, as there was no one present from the North. Was it, considering the circumstances in which it met, a free Assembly, at least in the old sense of the term? To one of its acts we shall refer immediately. The Revolution rights of the Scottish Church were fully secured in the Treaty of Union in 1707.

This Settlement of the Church divides the post-Reformation history of Scotland into two distinct periods. The Church occupied the place of that of Knox and Henderson. It was hardly identical with either. It had the Confession of the latter, and the form of worship of the Puritans. It was mediocre. There was no name of mark connected with it except that of William Carstairs, Principal of the University of Edinburgh, minister successively of Greyfriars and the High Church of that city, and the friend of King William. Cardinal Carstairs, as he has been called, was perhaps the best administrator the Church has ever had. The best thing we can say of the

Revolution Church is that she was the mother of churches (the present Establishment and her Non-Established sisters) better than herself. Had she Spiritual Independence? Dr. Taylor Innes points out that there were two parties within her, one contending she possessed legislative power, the other denying it. The question was not decided in the Courts of Law till one hundred and forty years later. If the youthful lives of Cameron and Renwick had been prolonged, would they have joined the Revolution Church? Would their names have appeared in the roll of the Moderators of the Assembly?

Some of their followers formed the Cameronian regiment, now the 26th of the line. They drove back the Highland host at Dunkeld after Killiecrankie; their beloved commander, the soldier poet, the youthful William Cleland of Douglas being killed in the conflict. Their first chaplain was Alexander Shields, the biographer of Renwick and author of the well-known *Hind Let Loose* and other works. He, Thomas Linning and

William Boyd, the ministers of the Society people, submitted to the General Assembly of 1690, the papers they presented not being read. Linning afterwards became minister of Lesmahagow, and died in 1733, and was followed there by a nephew and grandnephew, both bearing the name of Thomas. Boyd, who was the first to proclaim King William at Glasgow, died minister of Dalry, in Galloway, in 1741. Shields's life was a short one. After a brief ministry at St. Andrews he joined the unfortunate Darien expedition, and on the return voyage died of malignant fever, at Port Royal, Jamaica, in the fortieth year of his age, and sixteenth of his ministry, in the year 1700. He may be considered the first foreign missionary of the Church of Scotland.

Many of the Society people must have dropped into the National Church gradually. What proportion eventually did so there are no means of ascertaining. The bulk of them stood out, objecting to the Revolution Settlement for several reasons, specially the ignoring of the

The Reformed Presbyterians 25

Covenant, the fact that the sovereigns had not signed it, and the absence of the assertion of the Divine right of Presbytery, not to mention others to which we have already alluded. If they had had a prudent leader, and a sufficient supply of ministers and preachers, they would have exercised a powerful influence on the South of Scotland. They continued to hold their meetings in places like Leadhills, Crawfordjohn, Carnwath and Friarminon, then not easily accessible. Their societies and prayer meetings must have prepared the way for the success of the Seceders in the next generation. The one sowed, the other reaped.

So strongly attached were these men to Presbytery, that for fifteen years they waited for a regular ordained minister. without having the Lord's Supper dispensed and Baptism administered to their children. At length he appeared in the person of the Rev. John M'Millan. Born 1669, at Barncauchlaw, in the Parish of Minnigaff, in the Stewartry, and brought up among the Society people, he joined history is peculiar. Ordained Parish minister of Abbotshall he joined the Seceders, left them for the Cameronians, and eventually returned to the Establishment. Mr. M'Millan and he, with an elder, 1st August 1743, formed a Presbytery at Braehead, Dalserf, calling it the Reformed Presbytery. They then proceeded to ordain ministers.

M'Millan died at Broomhill, Bothwell, in the eighty-fourth year of his age and fifty-third of his ministry, on the last day of November 1753, within two days of completing forty-seven years' service among the Hillmen, and was buried in Dalserf churchyard. His friend, Mr. Charles Umpherston, surgeon, Pentland, states that his last words were "My Lord, my God, my Redeemer, yea mine own God is He," and adds, "After he had fully finished his Course with a pleasant Countenance, his Eyes lifted up, and his right Hand a little raised up to Heaven, he willingly resigned up his Soul to his beloved and faithful Saviour in that full Faith and firm Persuasion, that with his Eyes he should see his Redeemer, and not another for him." After him, his followers have been called M'Millanites.

The Church gradually grew. At the close of the XVIII century there were fourteen congregations. The Reformed Presbyterian Synod was formed in 1811. Among the earlier ministers were the four Johns—M'Millan, the son of the first M'Millan, Courtass, Thorburn, and Fairley; among the later, the Symingtons and the Goolds, not to mention others. These ministers, with slender incomes, command our admiration and respect for the consistent stand they made for their principles, and their efforts to maintain sound evangelical doctrine and practice. The Synod had its trials and small divisions. It founded congregations in Ireland and America. It latterly carried on successful missions in the new Hebrides, including among its agents the late Dr. John Inglis and the well-known Dr. John Paton. From time to time it issued Testimonies, which are in reality Declaratory Acts. In the edition of these, which was published in 1837-9, the doctrinal portion extended to one hundred and sixty-six, and the historical to two hundred and sixty-eight pages. In this we surely have Church first and Creed second; Spiritual independence first and State connection second.

CHAPTER III

THE SECESSION CHURCH, 1733-1847.

WE have discussed the first two dates on the cover of the United Free *Record*. These belong to the XVI and XVII, the remaining ones to the XVIII and XIX centuries. The first three of those later ones are dates of Separation, the second three of Union. We now pass to the separations. The story of the earlier centuries is more stirring and exciting than that of the later. It deals with fines, imprisonment, torture, martyrdoms, battles. The narrative of the others is occupied with contests in the Church and Civil Courts and sufferings of a milder nature, and therefore less known.

The year 1733 is connected with the Secession and the brothers Ebenezer and Ralph Erskine. Their names stand on the roll of the fathers of our Church next to M'Millan. They belonged to one of the oldest historic families, and could trace descent from the Earl of Mar, who was contemporary with Malcolm Canmore. They also had Stuart blood in their veins. Their father, Henry Erskine, was one of the two thousand ministers ousted in England on St. Bartholomew's day, 1662. Before the Revolution he preached at Whitsome, near Berwick, where he was the instrument of the conversion of Thomas Boston, the author of the *Fourfold State*. In his old age he was minister of Chirnside. His son Ebenezer was born on the day the Sanquhar Declaration was issued; Ralph four years later. We may note in passing that Ebenezer was the brother-in-law of the well-known Dr. Alexander Webster of Edinburgh, and Ralph was tutor of Mr. Erskine, the author of the *Institutes of the Law of Scotland*. The scene of their ministerial labours was in the counties immediately north of the Forth—Fife, Kinross, Stirling, the centre of the Secession.

The Secession Church

The greater portion of Ebenezer's ministry was spent in the quiet parish of Portmoak. He was translated to Stirling after he was fifty years of age. Ralph's ministerial life was spent in Dunfermline. The brothers were very different in disposition. The elder seems to have been strong-minded, calm, stately, self-possessed, a man of integrity and intrepidity. The younger was of a gentler nature, full of humour, a poet (as evidenced by his Sacred Songs), and a musician, often amusing himself with his violin. As preachers both excelled. Their sermons are still read. An ecclesiastical opponent said of Ebenezer, addressing a friend, "If you never heard Ebenezer Erskine preach, sir, you have not heard the Gospel in its majesty." Ralph excelled in illustration and appeal.

The occasion of the Secession was the preaching of a sermon by Ebenezer Erskine as Moderator of the Synod of Perth and Stirling, at Perth, on 10th October 1732, from the words, "The stone which the builders refused is become the head of the corner" (Psalm cxviii. 22). In it he denounced the defections of the times. What, it will be asked, were these defections? The Revolution Church had not the fervour and spiritual life of the Church of the Covenant. Carstairs, its representative man, was not the equal of Henderson. It had neither a Dickson nor a Rutherford. A lower spiritual life, mere doctrinal preaching, attendance on religious ordinances, and Puritan strictness in some departments of life were its characteristics. These not unnaturally degenerated into sleepy orthodoxy and formalism. There were cases of heresy. We need not enter into that of Professor Simson of Glasgow, the treatment of which by the Assembly did not satisfy several of the ministers of the day.

Another case must be noticed more in detail, for it influenced the future of the religious life of Scotland, and raised the question which is at present being discussed afresh, the warrant for the Gospel offer. In the middle of the preceding century there appeared in England

The Secession Church

a book entitled *The Marrow of Modern Divinity*, by E. F. These initials stand for Edward Fisher. Who Fisher was, the latest editor of his work leaves undecided. About seventy years later Thomas Boston found a copy of it in a cottage in the Parish of Simprin where he had begun his ministry. He read it and spoke of it to his friends. A new edition was published, edited by Hog of Carnock. The book is in the form of dialogues, discussing experiences put in the mouths of the speakers. It gave offence to many. Some of the statements were unguarded. Others, when separate from the context, were misunderstood. They related to the Extent of the Atonement, the Nature of Saving Faith, the Free Offer of the Gospel, and kindred topics. The book was condemned by the Assembly of 1720. A representation against this decision was presented to the following Assembly by twelve ministers, nicknamed the Twelve Apostles, and now known as the Marrow Men. Among them were Boston, Hog, and the

Erskines. They all were rebuked and admonished in 1722.

The other principal source of defection was the Restoration of the Law of Patronage in 1712. For some years the Act was almost a dead letter. When it came to be enforced, there was a lack of uniformity in the action taken by the Presbyteries. The Assembly supported the Patrons in the most of the cases that were appealed. When the Presbyteries refused to comply with its injunctions, Riding Commissions were appointed to carry out the ordinations and inductions. In the discussions on this subject the Erskines took part on the side of the people. When Ebenezer Erskine preached his sermon denouncing the defections of the Church, the Synod resolved to censure him, and he eventually appealed to the Assembly.

Both brothers were rebuked and admonished by the Supreme Court during its sittings in 1733; Ralph, on the forenoon of the 14th of May, with other members of the Dunfermline Presbytery, for an

The Secession Church

"unwarrantable" act on their part, the refusing to enter on their roll the name of Mr. Stark of Kinross, who had been recently settled there by a Riding Commission; Ebenezer, on the afternoon of the same day when his appeal was dismissed. The Assembly would not receive a protest signed by the elder Erskine and his friends. It was left on the table, picked up by Mr. Naismith of Dalmeny, and read. The brethren were then summoned to appear at the bar next day, the last of the Assembly, and commanded to appear before the Commission in August to confess their sorrow. The Assembly further enjoined the Commission, in the event of their refusal, to suspend them, and, if necessary, to proceed to other censures. In August they adhered to their protest, and accordingly were suspended. Disregarding their suspension, they were in November, by the casting vote of the Moderator, Dr. John Goldie, Professor of Divinity in, and afterwards Principal of the University of Edinburgh, loosed from their charges, which were declared vacant. After sentence, they read a protest in which they said "We are obliged to make a Secession . . . and appeal to the first Free, Faithful, and Reforming General Assembly of the Church of Scotland." The names adhibited are Ebenezer Erskine, William Wilson, Alexander Moncrieff, James Fisher. Mr. Wilson was one of the ministers of Perth, the first of the four to die; Mr. Moncrieff, the Laird of Culfargie and minister of Abernethy, and Mr. Fisher, minister of Kinclaven, afterwards of the first Secession Church in Glasgow. now Greyfriars, author with the Erskines of the well-known Catechism which bears his name, and son-in-law of the elder brother. All of these filled the office of Professor of Divinity.

These met on the 5th December 1733, at Gairney Bridge, three miles from Kinross, at "a quiet wayside inn," and on the following day formed themselves into a Presbytery. They were joined in 1737 by Ralph Erskine and Mair of Orwell, and later on by Nairn of Abbots-

The Secession Church

hall, and Thomson of Burntisland. For seven years the Seceders occupied an anomalous position. The Synod of Perth, in obedience to the Assembly of 1734, had restored them to their parishes, and other steps were taken to induce them to return to the National fold. They, however, remained firm, some will think obstinately so. For a time they took no agressive measures. Many applications were made to them by people in various parishes for ordinances. At length they complied to the best of their ability, taxing their strength to the uttermost, journeying without any of our modern conveniences, preaching, baptising, dispensing the Communion. They issued a Testimony, appointed a professor, licensed a student.

This state of things of course could not continue indefinitely. At length the Church of Scotland took action. The brethren were libelled. They appeared before the General Assembly on 17th May 1739 with their Moderator, Mr. Mair, at their head, who read their declinature, and they then withdrew. Two days later the Assembly resolved to delay finally disposing of the case for another year. In 1740, when called to the bar, they did not appear, and, on the 15th of May, sentence of deposition was in their absence pronounced upon them "in the name of the Lord Jesus Christ, the sole King and Head of the Church," the usual form, by the Moderator, Mr. George Logan, of the Trinity College Church, Edinburgh, the author of a book on Civil Government and the Protestant Succession, which involved him in a controversy with the well-known Thomas Ruddiman. Two days later Mr. Logan, in his concluding address, referred to "the hard law and grievance of patronage," and denounced, in strong terms, what he called "a most unwarrantable Secession."

Most of the Seceders were left undisturbed in the possession of their churches for some time. Moncrieff preferred preaching in the open air. Ebenezer Erskine, on the Lord's Day after the Assembly, found the gates of the town

The Secession Church

church closed. Carrying his Bible, he led the people to an eminence north of Stirling, and, after singing the first four verses of the 60th Psalm, and prayer, preached from Matthew viii. 27, "But the men marvelled, saying, What manner of man is this that even the winds and the sea obey Him." Wilson, on the same day, found the Magistrates of Perth drawn up in front of the church. Three times he demanded admission in the name of his Divine Master. When this was refused, he would allow no violence, and accepting the offer of the Glovers' yard, made by their deacon on the spot, he preached from Hebrews xiii. 13, "Let us go forth therefore unto Him without the camp bearing His reproach." At the close of the day he said to his daughter, then a girl of twelve, "Bell, this has been a day of trial, but we have reason to be thankful that it has not been a day of shame. If anyone asks you, Bell, why your father lost his kirk, you may just say, as good Mr. Guthrie before his death directed my mother to say of him if she was asked why he lost his head, that it was in a good cause." It should be explained that the mother of Wilson was the niece of the wife of the martyr.

The Seceders had contended for reforms within the Establishment, and had failed. If they had succeeded they would have endangered the Revolution Settlement, and brought the Church into collision with the Civil Courts, anticipating the decisions of a century later. Now they formed an independent ecclesiastical judicatory. They adhered to the English Westminster Confession, and elevated the Catechisms, Larger and Shorter, to the rank of Standards. This did not seem to satisfy them. For, two years after their final separation from the National Church, on the 28th of December 1743, at Stirling, they renewed the Covenants, fifteen ministers signing these documents, one of them from Sanquhar, another from Cambusnethan. Both the Erskines preached on this occasion. Ebenezer at the commencement from Isa. xxii. 24, "They shall hang upon Him all the glory of His

The Secession Church

Father's house," and Ralph at the close from Deut. xxvi. 17, 18, "Thou hast avouched the Lord this day to be thy God," etc. Four brethren who were absent signed later, and the Covenants were made terms of ministerial communion. Two years further on, a Synod was formed. This consisted of twenty-six ministers, with seventeen vacant charges, and was divided into three Presbyteries, Dunfermline, Glasgow, and Edinburgh. The last was the largest of these, one of its members being a minister from Lockerbie.

Two years later, the Breach occurred. It is unnecessary to enter into detail regarding the Burgess Oath. Suffice it to say, that at a meeting held in Bristo Church, Edinburgh, the Synod split in two on this question, on the 9th April 1747. The Erskines headed the Burghers, Moncrieff and Adam Gib the Anti-Burghers. The one party adopted the name of the Associate, the other of the General Associate Synod. The Anti-Burghers eventually deposed and excommunicated the Burghers, including, of course, the Erskines. Ralph's son John, and Ebenezer's son-in-law, Scot of Gateshaw, voted for the excommunication of their relatives. When Scot returned home, his wife said, "You have excommunicated my father and my uncle: you are my husband, but never now shall you be minister of mine." She kept her word, riding to the Burgher Church in Jedburgh.

Ralph survived the Breach five years, and died 6th November 1752, after a short illness, his last words being, "I shall be for ever a debtor to free grace; victory, victory, victory." When Ebenezer heard of his death he said, with great emotion, "And is Ralph gone? He has twice got the start of me, he was first in Christ and now is first in glory." Ebenezer lingered on for eighteen months in great weakness, and died peacefully, his hand under his cheek, on the morning of the 2nd June 1754, in the seventy-fourth year of his age and fifty-first of his ministry, within a year of his elder contemporary, M'Millan.

The Secession Church

Ebenezer Erskine must occupy a foremost place in the annals of the United Free Church. His faults were mainly those of his age. If he had possessed more of the geniality of his brother, and the power of organisation, he might have anticipated the work of Chalmers a century later. One word has been applied to his character. That word is dignity. It is true of him more than any other Scottish ecclesiastical leader, Henderson possibly excepted. He probably never asked himself the question, Creed first, Church second, or Church first, Creed second. The historian and biographer cannot say what his position was on this point. His preaching, and that of his compeers, was evangelical in the best sense. They preached a full and free gospel to their fellow-men. The Erskines never joined Mr. M'Millan, and the followers of each remained apart till 1900. Both parties signed the Covenants, but they differed on the relation of the Civil Magistrate to the mediator King. The older party desired a Covenanted

King, State, and Nation. The latter was loyal not only to the Revolution Settlement on its Civil side, but to the House of Hanover. They both placed Spiritual Independence first. State connection second. The Civil Magistrate was the barrier to union, and the occasion of the separation between Burgher and Anti-Burgher. The Breach should be spoken of with bated breath. The effects of the Erskines' work have been greater than they could have anticipated.

During the seventy-three years which elapsed till the Breach was healed, both branches of the Secession steadily grew. There was not a year, with the exception of 1811 and 1813, when there was not at least one congregation added to one or other of the Synods. The average increase was at the rate of nearly four per annum, the increase being greater in the Anti-Burgher Synod during the earlier part of the period, that in the Burgher during the later. Congregations were added from all parts of Scotland, from Orkney to Galloway, the Gaelic-speaking excepted. The strength of the Secession lay rather in the central and southern than in the northern counties. It would be impossible to name the numerous eminent and successful preachers and faithful pastors who are remembered in various parts of the country. It may be enough to record the fact that among the Professors of the Burgher section are to be reckoned John Brown of Haddington, the peasant lad who knew nearly one dozen languages, and has given Scotland the Self-Interpreting Bible, so common in the homes of our country people, the Bible Dictionary, and the Concordance; and the versatile Dr. George Lawson of Selkirk, who was credited with being able to repeat the Scriptures in the original languages, and whose expository volumes on books and characters of the Old Testament are still held in esteem. It may be mentioned that Brown was father of John of Whitburn, and Ebenezer of Inverkeithing. Among the students of the same Synod was the youthful Michael Bruce, in whose brief career and poetry an interest is still taken. Among the Anti-Burghers were to be found the erudite Dr. John Jamieson, the author of the *Scottish Dictionary*, *History of the Culdees*, and other works; the well-known Dr. Thomas M'Crie, the biographer of Knox and Melville; and Professor George Paxton, the author of *Illustrations of Scripture*. It is interesting to read the account of the efforts made by both sections to meet the applications for assistance from England, Ireland, and North America, where the descendants of those aided by the Seceders now form considerable portions of the various Presbyterian Churches.

Towards the close of their separate careers, both sections were engaged in disputes regarding the relation of the Church to the State and the Covenants, disputes which ended in division. Among the Burghers the occasion of this was the preparing of a Preamble to the Formula. Three ministers and three elders formed themselves into a Presbytery in 1799, and six years later,

The Secession Church

when the number of their ministers had amounted to fifteen, they formed themselves into the Original Associate Synod. Among the Anti-Burghers the occasion of the separation was the issuing of a new Testimony. Four ministers in 1806 formed themselves into the Constitutional Presbytery. All of them were deposed by the Anti-Burgher Synod. Among their number were Professor Archibald Bruce and the elder M'Crie. We will meet with these small sections further on.

The long separation was drawing to a close. The movement for union in a single Synod was commenced by laymen connected with the congregations of Mid-Calder, Anti-Burgher; and East Calder, Burgher, in 1818. Two years later it was consummated on 8th September 1820 in Bristo Church, the scene of the Breach of 1747. The processions consisted of ministers, elders, probationers, students. The members of the two churches sat in alternate pews. Dr. Jamieson, the Moderator of the Anti-Burghers, commenced the proceedings by giving out Psalm cii. 17-22. After the minutes were read, and the Moderators had declared the Synods one, Dr. Jamieson and Mr. Balmer of Berwick (afterwards Professor), gave each other the right hand of fellowship, in which they were followed by the members present. Thereafter Mr. David Greig of Lochgelly, Burgher, the oldest minister in the Synod, ordained over fifty years earlier, and then nearly seventy years of age (the life-long friend of Professor Lawson, who had died seven months earlier), was elected Moderator. The devotional exercises that followed were concluded by the immense audience singing the opening verses of Psalm cxlvii., and the first Union was completed. An old man from Glasgow, who had witnessed the Separation, was present. So interested was he in the healing of the Breach that he had not slept for several nights. At the Union, the Burgher ministers numbered one hundred and thirty-nine, the Anti-Burghers one hundred and twenty-three. The United Church adopted the name of the United

The Secession Church

Associate Synod of the Secession Church.

In the following year a few brethren belonging to the Anti-Burgher section, including Professor Paxton and the Rev. George Stevenson of Ayr, author of works on the Atonement and the Offices of Christ, not satisfied with the new attitude of the Synod regarding the Covenants and the Testimony, withdrew and formed a Presbytery. Six years later, on 17th May 1827, they united with the Constitutional Presbytery, under the designation of the Original Secession Synod, thus claiming to be the true representatives of the Erskines.

The United Associate Synod, during the twenty-seven years of its separate existence, continued to increase in numbers and influence. It included among its ministers many who stood high in their day as preachers and pastors. Among its Professors were ranked Dr. John Dick, author of a treatise on Inspiration, and four volumes of Divinity Lectures; and Dr. John Brown, of Broughton Place,

Edinburgh, the first Scottish exegete of his generation, and author of several Commentaries and volumes of Expository Lectures, the grandson of Brown of Haddington, and father of Dr. John Brown, the well-known author of *Rab and his Friends*, and of the present Professor of Chemistry in the University of Edinburgh. The Synod started missions in Jamaica and Western Africa. The outstanding event in its history was the Atonement Controversy, which led to the only Scottish Secession of any size which was unconnected with the Church and State question. The youthful and able James Morison of Kilmarnock, one of the best Bible scholars Scotland has produced, along with his father and two friends, who were extruded from the Synod, along with some elders, formed the Evangelical Union in the same week that the Free Church separated from the State. This sect has prospered, but the majority of it in 1896 joined the Congregational Union. We should mention that the United Associate Synod adopted a new Testi-

The Secession Church

mony, which, like some others we have referred to, occupied a position somewhat similar to that of the more modern Declaratory Acts. During this period the views of the majority of the Synod materially changed on the relations between Church and State. What are known as Voluntary views spread rapidly among them.

CHAPTER IV.

THE RELIEF CHURCH, 1752-1847.

WE have now to retrace our steps from the forties of last century to the second date of Separation on the cover of our *Record*, 1761, the year of the formation of the Presbytery of Relief — indeed, to 1752, nine years earlier still. The Relief is associated with the name of Thomas Gillespie, who stands next to the Erskines and the Seceding brethren in the succession of the founders of the United Free Church. Inferior to them in ability, he was second to none of them in the gentler graces of the Christian character. He reminds us in this respect more of Renwick than of any other who went before him. His early life prepared him for his later work. Brought up by a godly mother near Edinburgh, he was taken by her to hear the elder Boston at a communion at Galashiels; and, having come under the force of the truth, studied for the ministry. Near the close of his studies he spent ten days at the Secession Hall, but left it. He then went to Doddridge's Seminary at Northampton, where he would mix with young men belonging to the Baptists, Independents, and other bodies. He was ordained there on the 22nd of January 1741 by dissenting ministers, Doddridge presiding. On 4th September, in the same year, he was inducted to the parish of Carnock (the second successor to Hog, who had edited the *Marrow of Modern Divinity*), in the Presbytery of Dunfermline, little more than a year after Ralph Erskine had been cut off from its membership. In signing the Confession of Faith, he made an explanation regarding the power of the Civil Magistrate.

Here, apparently, a quiet and uneventful ministry awaited him. But it was not so to be. The troubles in the Church occasioned by the administration of the Law of Patronage had not been removed. The Assembly had not found a uniform course of action in the settlement of ministers. In 1751 the Presbytery of Linlithgow had been censured for not placing a minister at Torphichen, and the settlement was eventually carried out by a Riding Commission, the last that was appointed. On it were found, among others, the names of Logan, who had pronounced the sentence of deposition upon the Erskines; Hugh Blair, author of the celebrated Sermons; Robertson, the historian; Home, the author of *Douglas;* the Solicitor-General of the day; and the Lord Provost of Edinburgh. Robertson, then minister of Gladsmuir, who had made his first speech in the Assembly in connection with the case, was appointed to preach and preside at the ordination.

The case of Inverkeithing was then pending. Mr. Richardson of Broughton, in Peeblesshire, had been presented. The people were opposed to him. The case had been before the Supreme Court in

1750-1. The Presbytery of Dunfermline had refused to induct the presentee, although instructed to do so by the Commission of November 1751. When the Assembly met in the following year, Dr. Patrick Cuming, Professor of Church History in the University of Edinburgh, one of the ministers of the Old Church in that city, the leader of the Moderate party, who had been Moderator three years earlier, was re-elected to the chair. The Assembly was determined to enforce subordination on the inferior courts. The Presbytery was enjoined to meet at Inverkeithing on Thursday, 21st May, for the induction, five instead of three to form a quorum. To order a Presbytery to discharge this duty during the sitting of the Assembly, and to enlarge the quorum, were unusual acts.

On the Friday, when the Presbytery reappeared at the bar, it was found only three had attended and no induction had taken place. Six of the brethren stood firm. It was resolved one of them should be deposed the next day. They were dealt with individually. Gillespie, who was called in last, read a humble representation, which was not received. The vote was then taken—the majority of the members did not take part in it. About a third of the Assembly voted for Gillespie—fifty-two in all—most of them being elders. He was solemnly deposed in the usual manner. When he heard the sentence, he said, "Moderator, I desire to receive this sentence of the General Assembly of the Church of Scotland pronounced against me with real concern and awful impressions of the Divine conduct in it: but I rejoice that to me it is given, in behalf of Christ, not only to believe on Him, but also to suffer for His sake." This sentence was, to say the least of it, high-handed and extreme. Subordination might have been enforced by inflicting a lighter one. We should add that, for not attending the induction of Mr. Richardson a few weeks later, three other members of Presbytery were suspended from their functions in the Church Courts, their own Sessions excepted, and the sentence remained in force for twelve years. It must be remembered that in these proceedings the Civil Courts were not appealed to by any party. The action taken was that of the Church.

After receiving his sentence, Gillespie returned to Carnock, and told his wife when she met him in front of the manse, "I am no longer minister of Carnock." She nobly replied, "Well, if we must beg, I will carry the meal-pock." The next day he preached, in the open air, a Gospel sermon from the words, 1 Cor. ix. 16, "Necessity is laid upon me, yea, woe is unto me if I preach not the Gospel." A place of worship was soon made ready for him in Dunfermline. He does not seem to have denounced the Church that had condemned him, but he did not personally seek restoration. His friends made a strong effort in that direction in the Assembly of 1753, but were defeated by a small majority of three votes.

Thomas Gillespie did not join the Reformed Presbyterians or the Seceders.

He did not bind himself by signing the Covenant. For fully six years he stood alone, doing his work without ministerial assistance. At communion seasons he would preach eight or nine sermons, and deliver nearly as many table addresses. These sermons seemed to have been fully written out and outlines of the addresses were prepared.

At length help arrived. The congregation of Jedburgh desired to have Thomas Boston of Oxnam, the son of the author of *The Fourfold State*, for their minister. The patron did not present him. Mr. Boston and the congregation separated from the Establishment. On 9th December 1757 he was inducted. The bells rang. The Magistrates and Council, with their insignia of office, walked in procession to the new church, and Mr. Roderick Mackenzie, from England, presided. At Boston's second communion Mr. Gillespie assisted. During the action sermon Gillespie sat weeping like a child.

Three years after the foundation of the congregation at Jedburgh, the parishioners

The Relief Church

of Kilconquhar, in Fife, felt dissatisfied with the presentation to Dr. John Chalmers of Elie, grand-uncle of Thomas Chalmers. They consulted Gillespie, who preached to them and administered baptism. A congregation was formed in Colinsburgh, and Mr. Thomas Colier, a minister from England, was chosen pastor. He was inducted on 22nd October 1761, Boston preaching on the occasion. Thereafter, the three ministers, with three elders, one of whom was Provost of Dunfermline, formed the Presbytery of Relief. Their minute is very interesting, but too long for insertion here. In it is no mention of Confession, Covenant, or Testimony. The Presbytery rest on the Scriptures, own the Redeemer as Head of the Church, and declare themselves Presbyterians. Here we have again Spiritual Independence first, the Civil Magistrate not named. Have we not also Church first, Creed second? Ministers from the Establishment, the Secession, and the Reformed Presbyterians, in Scotland, and from England, joined the Relief. In 1772 a and State were from the first advanced, and ignored the Revolution Settlement. We cannot estimate too highly the debt that Scotland owes to the followers of the Erskines and Gillespie. They kept alive spiritual religion in many a remote corner of the country, as well as in large cities, by faithful doctrinal preaching. They laboured in season and out of season among their flocks, scattered over wide districts. They were the friends of civil and religious liberty, latterly of Sabbath Schools and Temperance Societies. Their history always reminds us of the words of the Prophet of the Restoration: "Who hath despised the day of small things?" and those of an earlier one: "A little one shall become a thousand and a small one a strong nation."

CHAPTER V.

THE TEN YEARS' CONFLICT, 1834-1843.

WE now turn to the third Separation date on the cover of the *Record*—1843. This brings us to contemporary history. A few of those who took part in the events of this period are still among the living. Most elderly people can recall some incidents of the time. It suggests comparison and contrast with what had preceded. We are now on different ground, in a different atmosphere.

The year 1843 will be for ever associated with the name of Thomas Chalmers. He stands next in order of time to Gillespie among the founders of our Church. He was a native, like Henderson and Cameron, of the county of Fife, the county where Ralph Erskine and Gillespie laboured. His father was a general merchant in the town of Anstruther. Thomas, the sixth child and fourth son in a family of fourteen, was born one hundred years after Ebenezer Erskine. He was a lad of "pregnant pairts," and was licensed at the early age of nineteen. He was versatile, genial, sympathetic, earnest, full of enthusiasm, a born orator, a devoted pastor, a large hearted Catholic Christian. He was a candidate for Professorships of Mathematics and Natural Philosophy and occupied the Chair of Moral Philosophy in St. Andrews, and that of Divinity in Edinburgh. He wrote on Philosophical, Social and Political questions, and on Natural and Dogmatic Theology, and published sermons and expository discourses. Like Henderson and Ebenezer Erskine he did not come under the saving power of the truth till he had been some years in the ministry. His first charge was Kilmany, in his native county, half way between Cupar and Newport-on-Tay. When minister of the Tron and of St. John's, Glasgow, he began the work that made him the father of Home Missions and Church Extension, both of which had been notoriously neglected by the Church of Scotland. As a leader, Chalmers occupied a different position from M'Millan, the Erskines and Gillespie. They stood single-handed or nearly so, contending for what they considered the truth. He was the leader of a party of which he had been a member, and was aided by able coadjutors, clerical and lay.

The party known by that elastic and much-abused word "Moderate" and led successively by Principal Robertson of Edinburgh, the historian, Principal Hill of St. Andrews, the author of *Lectures on Divinity*, Dr. John Inglis of Edinburgh, and Dr. George Cook of St. Andrews, who had guided the business of the Assembly for fully half a century, were gradually losing their influence early in the XIX century. The popular and more evangelical party, that of Webster, John Erskine the colleague of Robertson, the first Sir Henry Moncreiff and Andrew Thomson, all of Edinburgh, men of equal ability and culture, was gaining ground. With the new century there was a greater interest in religious subjects. The tide may be said to have turned when Andrew Thomson became minister of the New Greyfriars, Edinburgh, and the leading preacher in the capital. His new church of St. George's, in the west end, was filled by the *élite* of the city. His second successor in it was Robert Candlish, the successor of Chalmers as a church leader. In 1829, Alexander Duff sailed as the first missionary of the Church of Scotland for India. In 1831, the Assembly deposed Campbell of Row for heresy in statements as to the extent of the atonement and the nature of faith. In connection with this case, William Cunningham, then of Greenock, the successor of Chalmers as a theological teacher, made his first public appearance as a witness before the Presbytery of Dumbarton. Shortly after, he succeeded, as minister of the Trinity College Church, Edinburgh, Mr. Tait, who was deposed for holding the views of Campbell.

The Ten Years' Conflict 69

The age was that of Catholic emancipation, abolition of slavery, electoral and municipal reform. The Voluntaries, including many belonging to the Secession and Relief, were agitating for the separation of Church and State. It was felt that the Church must be popularised. Chalmers and other Evangelical leaders were Conservatives in politics, and for reasons which we cannot now take time to state resolved not to seek from Parliament the removal of Patronage but to rest upon "The Call." Overtures on the subject were tabled in the Assembly of 1832 but were rejected. A motion made by Chalmers in the following year was lost by a majority of twelve. Now commenced what is known as the Ten Years' Conflict, 1834-43. It is thought by many, and not unnaturally, it might have been averted if Drs. Inglis and Andrew Thomson had been spared a few years longer. The former died on the second day of 1834. The latter dropped down dead on his own doorstep two years earlier.

The Revolution Settlement was now to receive an exact legal interpretation from the Courts of Law. Chalmers was in his fifty-fourth year, of the same age as Ebenezer Erskine when the Secession Presbytery was formed at Gairney Bridge a century earlier. He was greatly aided by a band of able young men who had been ordained within the ten preceding years, Cunningham, Robert Buchanan of Glasgow, James Begg, afterwards of Edinburgh, and others.

The Assembly of 1834 passed two memorable Acts, the Veto and the Chapel. Both of these were carried by majorities—the one by 184 to 139, the other by 152 to 103. The former declared that if the majority of the heads of families in a vacant congregation object to the presentee without reason assigned, the Presbytery were not to proceed with the settlement. Its supporters were thenceforth known as Non-Intrusionists. They had been warned by many outside and inside the Establishment that the step was illegal, and the two chief Judges of the

Supreme Court, who were elders in the Assembly, voted against the measure. Several sound lawyers had, however, given advice to the contrary. It is probable that, if the consequences had been foreseen, the Act might not have been proposed. The Chapel Act authorised the Presbyteries to assign parishes *Quoad Sacra* to Chapel of Ease ministers, and recognised the right of these ministers to seats in the Church Courts. The Assembly of 1836 placed in the Moderator's Chair one of that class of ministers, Dr. Norman Macleod of the Gaelic Chapel, Glasgow, afterwards known as St. Columba's. The only other *Quoad Sacra* minister on whom the Church of Scotland has as yet bestowed this honour is his son, Dr. Donald Macleod of the Park Church, Glasgow, who presided in 1895. The Moderator-Designate for 1906, Dr. Thomas Niven, Pollokshields, Glasgow, is also one.

The Veto Act worked well. In five years it was put in force in only ten instances. One of these was the case of

Auchterarder. In October 1834, the Patron, the Earl of Kinnoul, presented to that parish Mr. Robert Young. He was vetoed by two hundred and eighty-seven heads of families, only three names being adhibited to the call. The Presbytery rejected the presentation, and all appeals to the General Assembly were dismissed. The Patron and the Presentee raised an action in the Court of Session. The case, perhaps the most important of modern times, was heard before the whole court, an unusual proceeding. The pleadings occupied three weeks. The senior counsel for the Patron and Presentee was the Dean of Faculty, Mr. John Hope, afterwards Lord-Justice Clerk, and for the Presbytery, the Solicitor-General, Mr. Andrew Rutherfurd, afterwards Lord Rutherfurd. The opinions of the Judges took ten days to deliver. The judgment was given on the 8th of March 1838. Eight out of thirteen gave their opinions in favour of Mr. Young, including the two chiefs of the Court, who, as we have seen, had voted in the Assembly against the Veto. The five in favour of the Presbytery were Lord Glenlee, who had then been upwards of forty years on the bench, thus, perhaps, representing the judges of the XVIII century, and the well-known Whig lawyers—Fullarton, Moncreiff, Jeffrey and Cockburn. This decision, of course, was appealed against. The House of Lords confirmed it on 2nd May 1839, thus practically declaring the Veto Act beyond the power of the Assembly and illegal. The Presbytery did not take Mr. Young on trials for ordination. The House of Lords three years later found them liable in damages. The Presentee to Auchterarder was not settled till after May 1843.

Contemporary with this case was a second. Into it certain legal technicalities enter. Upon these we need not dwell. The circumstances were substantially as follows. The Crown, as Patron, presented a Mr. Clark as assistant and successor to the minister of Lethendy, which, like Auchterarder, is in Perthshire, the county wherein three of the first four Seceders had laboured. Mr. Clark was vetoed, and the Presbytery of Dunkeld rejected the presentation. Shortly afterwards the old minister died, and the Crown issued a second presentation in favour of Mr. Kessen. Mr. Clark appealed to the Court of Session for interdict, and that Court forbade the Presbytery to ordain. They, acting on the advice of the Commission of Assembly, proceeded to do so. Eight ministers, including Mr. Kessen, appeared before the Court, and were rebuked by the Lord President on the 17th of June 1839. Several of the Judges were disposed to imprison them.

A third case must be referred to. Not only did the Civil Court interdict the Presbytery from ordaining, but it enjoined this one to admit a minister. The Patron of Marnoch, in the Presbytery of Strathbogie, presented Mr. Edwards, a former assistant to the deceased minister, in September 1837. He had been unpopular, and his call was signed by only three heritors out of thirteen and a single parishioner. Peter Taylor by name, the keeper of a public-house where the Presbytery occasionally dined. The Presentee was rejected. Mr. Edwards appealed to the Court of Session. When the majority of the Presbytery, seven in number, resolved to comply with the orders of the Court the Commission of the Assembly suspended them. They disregarded this sentence and continued to officiate in their parishes, and eventually they ordained Mr. Edwards on the 21st of January 1841. Deep snow covered the ground. The members of Presbytery, five in number, who were to take part in the work of the day, and their advisers, arrived at Marnoch in carriages drawn by four horses. One of the lawyers present had to break a window in the manse before an entrance into it could be obtained. Hundreds of people from the parishes around journeyed on foot to be present on the occasion. They filled the gallery and gathered round the building. The parishioners filled the area of the church. Their agent addressed several questions to Mr. Thomson of Keith, who presided. When asked for his mandate he turned to the people, and in reply to his query whether he had their warrant to act for them they answered in the affirmative. He then read a protest, and followed by his clients, who had lifted their Bibles, left the church. Their places were quickly taken by those outside. A scene of riot and confusion ensued which was only quelled by a magistrate. Then Mr. Thomson preached and conducted the ordination service, Mr. Edwards responding in the usual manner to the questions addressed to him. The day's work has been described as an outrage and a scandal. A new place of worship was shortly after erected for the parishioners in a village three miles distant. There Mr. Henry was ordained minister by the four members of the Strathbogie Presbytery who adhered to the party of the majority of the Assembly.

The seven were deposed by the Assembly of 1841. Those who were sent to preach in their parishes by the Assembly were interdicted by the Court

The Ten Years' Conflict 77

of Session. They avoided the churches, but otherwise the interdicts were disregarded and these were not enforced. The ministers who assisted the seven at communions were suspended from their spiritual functions in Church Courts for a few months. The assistance, however, was still rendered.

Other cases of collision between the Civil and Ecclesiastical Courts occurred, but it is unnecessary to refer to them. During this period the General Assembly passed, by majorities, resolutions asserting the Spiritual Independence of the Church. Negotiations were carried on with both political parties, the Whig Government of Viscount Melbourne, the Tory of Sir Robert Peel. Bills, such as those of the Earl of Aberdeen and the Duke of Argyll, were brought into Parliament. All was without success. One difficulty that could not be overcome was the resolute attitude of the Church.

These movements not unnaturally suggest a comparison with those of 1733 and 1751. The principles were the same, but there was a difference. In one of the earlier cases eight men, in the other one man contended against the majority of the Assembly on account of the alleged defections of the Church. This time the Church, through the majority of the Assembly, contended with the Courts of Law, the Government, and the Legislature, for what she considered her inherent rights guaranteed to her, as she believed, by the Act of 1592, the Revolution Settlement and the Treaty of Union. The movement was similar to that of the Covenanters. In fact it might be called the Covenant in miniature. It was looked upon as a battle for the Redeemer's Crown.

Throughout, the leaders were supported by a large portion of the people. It was a period of religious revival. There was a religious movement in Dundee under the saintly M'Cheyne, not to mention others. We quote an impartial witness. The late Lord-Justice Clerk Moncreiff, in a preface he wrote to an edition of his brother's, the late Sir Henry

Moncreiff's, Chalmers Lectures says: "What the people wished to secure was the faithful preaching of the Word, administration of ordinances, and exercise of discipline. . . . The attachment to the leaders of the Evangelical party in the Church sprang from their Evangelical teaching." The people, too, felt that the conflict for non-intrusion was also for popular rights.

The Church's work was carried on energetically in every department. Additional missionaries were sent out to India. One of them is still (1906) spared to us, the venerable and venerated Dr. Thomas Smith. The Jewish Mission was founded. The discussions with the Voluntaries were carried on, but not in the best spirit on either side. Dr. Chalmers's Extension Scheme proved a great success. In four years, nearly two hundred churches were erected, at the cost of upwards of two hundred thousand pounds, raised voluntarily.

Another interesting result of the alterations introduced into the administration of the Church of Scotland was the union with the Mother Church of the Associate Synod of Original Burgher Seceders or Old Light Burghers, who, as we have already seen, separated from the Burghers in 1799. They had opened negotiations with the Old Light Anti-Burghers, but these had failed on account of the old obstacle, the Burgess Oath. After the passing of the Veto Act, a letter was addressed to the Moderator of the General Assembly intimating a desire on the part of the Synod to return to the Establishment. In the Assembly of 1835, the question of union was debated. The Moderates opposed it on constitutional grounds as *ultra vires*, and declined to act on the committee that was appointed to confer with the Burghers. The Union Act was passed in 1839. The Church recognised that the Seceders held the Establishment principle, and at the same time concurred with them in the necessity in particular circumstances of entering into solemn engagements for church defence. We may ask in passing, did this Act, carried by the Non-Intrusionists, make the holding of the Doctrine of Establishment a term of office? This Act contained eight regulations dealing with the admission of the ministers and congregations of the Burghers by the Presbyteries, and other practical details.

The mode of carrying out this Union was peculiar. The Synod, at its last meeting held on 31st July 1839, approved of the union, passing seven resolutions by 37 to 12, and empowered the Moderator, the Rev. John Wright of Alloa, to dissolve the Synod. Each minister was expected to apply individually to the Presbytery of the Church of Scotland within whose bounds he resided, and that Presbytery was empowered by the General Assembly to admit him. In entering into this Union, they acted on the lines of that protest which Ebenezer Erskine and his three brethren handed in to the General Assembly of 1733, wherein they "appeal to the first Free, Faithful, and Reforming General Assembly of the Church of Scotland." The question of the covenants was not insisted on, partly, we suppose, because it was not referred to in the original protest of Ebenezer Erskine and his three brethren in the Commission of March 1733, the signing of them having taken place, as we have already seen, after their final separation from the Establishment. The last of their seven resolutions is so remarkable that we insert it in full. "That inasmuch as a minority of the Synod may not yet see their way clear to accede to the Union in the meantime, the Synod desires to regard with all Christian consideration any difficulties that may be in their path; and, understanding that these brethren contemplate to act still in an associated capacity, the Synod, while not merging its powers as a Synod in the minority, do leave the books of Synod and of Presbyteries in their hands, with authority to take all use of them consistent with their remaining the property of the majority, in common with the minority, and so as to be accessible to them when required; and do not object to their taking the designation of the Associate Presbytery : or. if they see cause, of the

Associate Synod, while maintaining the common interests of truth and of attained-to reformation in the manner they prefer. And the majority and minority shall both be understood as pledging themselves to encourage no violent proceedings affecting the conscientious liberty of one another; nor litigations in respect of civil property; and that in case of any difficulties arising in questions of that kind, the same shall be settled by Christian arbitration." This resolution manifests such a Christian and brotherly spirit, that it may be said to have created a precedent for those engaged in similar courses of action.

Of the twelve members who stood out against the Union, two speedily followed their brethren to the Establishment, one eventually joined the Reformed Presbyterian Church, and another the United Associate Synod. The remainder in 1842 joined the old Light Anti-Burghers. The most marked man among those who joined the Establishment was Dr. Michael Willis of Glasgow, who afterwards became Principal of Knox's College. Toronto, and left his impress on the Canadian Church. Another of them, the Rev. James Clelland of Stewarton, was the occasion of the legality of the Chapel Act being brought under review in the Court of Session, when the Presbytery of Irvine, in obedience to the Assembly, received him as a member of Presbytery, and assigned him a district *Quoad Sacra*. Mr. Cunningham of Lainsaw, and other heritors, applied for and obtained interdict. When this was disregarded, the whole question was brought before the Court. It was pleaded before the thirteen judges. The decision was given on the 20th January 1843, and the Chapel Act, declaring chapel ministers members of Presbytery, was pronounced *ultra vires* by eight to five, the minority being the same judges as in the Auchterarder case, with the exception that Lord Ivory took the place of his predecessor, Lord Glenlee. This judgment was not appealed against; but its validity was recognised by the Parliament of 1844, when it passed an Act which permitted the erection of

The Ten Years' Conflict 85

Quoad Sacra parishes. Before we leave the Court of Session, we shall quote the words of one of the Lords. Lord Cockburn has written in his Journal that "if the Court of Session had fired interdicts into the Church in Robertson's time, as it has done lately, the Principal would have headed his whole battalion of Moderates in charges on the Court."

Before the judgment in the Stewarton case had been pronounced, the Non-Intrusion majority had taken two decided steps which we must briefly notice—the passing of the Claim of Right and the holding of the Convocation. The Claim, Declaration and Protest of the General Assembly of the Church of Scotland was brought into the Assembly of 1842 by overture from about one hundred and fifty members of that body. It was drawn up by Alexander Murray Dunlop, advocate, afterwards legal adviser of the Free Church, an office which he held till his death in 1870, and for which he declined to draw salary. He was a gentleman of whose character everyone, friend and opponent alike, spoke in the highest terms. The document has been called the new Solemn League and Covenant, its author, the modern Warriston. Dr. Chalmers having moved its adoption, and Dr. Gordon, of the High Church, Edinburgh, the Moderator of the preceding Assembly, having seconded, it was carried by 241 to 110, the other party meeting it by a series of resolutions. The Claim contains a statement founded on the Standards of the Church, the Acts of Assembly, and the Statutes of the Realm in support of Spiritual Independence, with an account of the proceedings of the Civil Courts by which these had been violated. In conclusion, it clearly indicates that if the wrongs complained of are not redressed, the alternative must be the loss of the temporal benefits of the Establishment, and expresses the hope that Almighty God "in His own good time would restore to them these benefits." This document is a defence by its authors of the interpretation put by them (as by the Erskines and Gillespie and their supporters in 1733 and 1752, without and within the Establishment) on the Revolution Settlement and Treaty of Union, and it places Spiritual Independence first and State connection second. When consenting to transmit the Claim to the Queen, the Royal Commissioner, the Marquis of Bute, stated that he expressed no approval of it. He sent it to Sir James Graham, the Home Secretary, who, in his reply to the Marquis, concurred emphatically with him. We should add, in this connection, that, by 216 to 147, the Assembly, on the motion of Mr. William Cunningham, afterwards Principal, passed a resolution for the abolition of Patronage.

The Convocation met in Edinburgh, November 1842. The circular calling it was signed by thirty-two of the oldest ministers in the Church, including Drs. Chalmers, Welsh, Grey, Gordon of Edinburgh, Thomas Brown, Paterson and Smyth of Glasgow, and Macfarlan of Greenock. The immediate occasion of its being summoned was the second Auchterarder decision, in which the

House of Lords held the Patron and Presentee of Auchterarder entitled to damages from the Presbytery for their not proceeding to take Mr. Young on trials. The proceedings commenced on Thursday, 17th November, the day after the ordinary meeting of the Commission of the Assembly, in St. George's Church, when the large building was filled to overflowing, and Dr. Chalmers preached a solemn and appropriate sermon on the words: "Unto the upright there ariseth light in the darkness," Psalm cxii. 4. On the following day, the brethren assembled in the Roxburgh Church, once a Relief place of worship, now Lady Glenorchy's Parish Church, situated in the south side of Edinburgh. No layman was admitted, no authentic record was preserved. One or two reports, more or less perfect, have been printed since. Four hundred and sixty-five ministers were present from all parts of the country—north, south, east, and west. There was free and frank discussion. The Convocation broke up on the 24th, after sitting a week. Two series of resolutions, five in each, were adopted, one dealing with the grievance, the other with the remedy. These went over substantially the same ground as the Claim of Right, and committed those who signed them to leave the Establishment if they did not obtain redress. The first series was signed by four hundred and twenty-three ministers, the second by three hundred and fifty-four. A memorial, embodying the resolutions, was also transmitted to Her Majesty's Government.

On the 4th of January 1843, the Home Secretary sent an elaborate answer to the addresses of the previous Assembly, in which he characterised the Church's claims as unreasonable. Dr. Welsh, as Moderator, on receiving it, called a *pro-re-nata* meeting of Commission for the 31st of the same month. At that meeting it was resolved to lay the Claim of Right before both Houses of Parliament. It was brought before the House of Commons, on the 10th of February, by the Honourable Fox Maule, afterwards Lord Panmure and Earl of Dalhousie, the Secretary for War during the Crimean conflict, and eventually a loyal elder of the Free Church. On the 7th of March he moved in the Lower House for the appointment of a Committee of Inquiry. He spoke for two hours with moderation and ability, and was supported by Mr. Rutherfurd, who, as we have seen, had acted as counsel for the Church in the Civil Courts; Sir George Grey, afterwards Home Secretary; and others. Among the speakers on the other side were the Home Secretary, Lord John, afterwards Earl Russell, then leader of the Opposition, later on Prime Minister, and Sir Robert Peel.

The debate lasted two days, and was carried on in a comparatively thin House. The motion was lost by 211 to 76, a majority of 135; out of the 37 Scots members present, 25 voted with Mr. Maule. In the minority, besides Sir George Grey, were Mr. Cobden and Mr. Milner Gibson. The Claim was not laid on the table of the House of Lords. A series of resolutions on the question, not favourable to high views of Spiritual Independence, was moved there by Lord Campbell, afterwards Lord Chancellor, and after a debate in which several Law Lords took part, was withdrawn.

CHAPTER VI.

THE PROTEST—THE EXODUS—THE DEED OF DEMISSION, MAY 1843.

THE Ten Years' Conflict may be said to have been ended by the events recorded at the close of the preceding chapter. Into it the Church's relation to the Confession did not enter. Neither did any doctrinal question. Evangelical teaching pervaded both parties, but there was little sympathy between the extreme members of each. It turned, as we have seen, on the old question of State connection; and it was not as on former occasions between two sections of the Church, but between the majority of the Assembly and the State. It is easy to be wise after the event, to say that all parties, statesmen, lawyers, moderates, and non-intrusionists made mistakes,

The Protest

and to endeavour to point these out. But on this we cannot now dwell. The Revolution Settlement was at last interpreted, interpreted by the Law Courts, Scots and English; by the British Parliament, Lords and Commons; by the two political parties, Tory and Whig; by the ministry representing the Crown. Their interpretation was not that of the Erskines, Gillespie, Chalmers and their supporters and sympathisers. It went far to justify the Hillmen for standing aloof from the Church of the Parliament of King William. The die was cast. The last act of the drama had to be performed. This was not the deposition of eight men in their absence, or the cutting off of an individual standing alone against an Assembly, but the separation of a large body of men from the State Establishment by their own act, under constraint of conscience and of the view they held of the Crown Rights of the Mediator King.

That event took place on the memorable 18th of May. one hundred and three years and three days after the deposition of the Erskines, four days short of ninety-one years after the extrusion of Gillespie. Few people, perhaps none, knew exactly what would occur. We have already referred, in our opening sentences, to the Commissioner's levée and the incident that happened at it, an incident emblematic of much that has followed and may yet follow. After his levée, the Marquis of Bute, according to custom, drove to the High Church within St. Giles' Cathedral, where the customary sermon at the opening of the Assembly was preached by the retiring Moderator. The church was crowded. The pulpit was occupied by Dr. David Welsh, Professor of Church History in the University of Edinburgh, a native of the Parish of Moffat, formerly minister at Crossmichael, in Galloway, and St. David's, Glasgow, one of the most cultured and catholic-minded men in the Church, who died two years later, aged fifty-two, and has been too quickly forgotten. His text was: "Let every man be fully persuaded in his own mind,"

Rom. xiv. 5. The clear and forcible sermon was full of allusion to the later events of the day.

About half-past two in the afternoon the proceedings of what perhaps was the most memorable General Assembly held since 1638 commenced in St. Andrew's Church, George Street, which was filled in every corner, many having been there for hours before. Near the Commissioner were the Lord Advocate, afterwards Lord Colonsay, Sir James Forrest, Lord Provost of Edinburgh, and others. After a brief prayer, the Moderator addressed a few preliminary observations to the Court, which technically was not yet constituted, and then, in impressive tones, amid unbroken silence, read the Protest, signed by two hundred and three members, of whom upwards of seventy were elders, —including the celebrated Sir David Brewster, several landed proprietors, advocates, writers to the signet and merchants of the west. This document was a protest against the rejection of the Claim of Right by the Legislature, and the signatories held that that Claim set forth the true constitution of the Church, and that the Assembly now called was not a free and lawful one. The final paragraph asserted the "right and duty of the Civil Magistrate to support an Establishment of religion in accordance with God's Word," and maintained the right of the signatories, and that of those adhering to them, to separate from the present Establishment, taking with them the Confession of Faith as the standard of the Church as heretofore understood. Dr. Welsh then laid the document upon the table, and bowing respectfully to the Commissioner, lifted his hat, and in gown and bands left the building. He was followed by Dr. Chalmers and other fathers of the Church. Then slowly and steadily those occupying the left side of the house, and several that had been seated on the cross benches, withdrew, accompanied by a section of the spectators. Many who remained looked on with astonishment and dismay at the number of those who thus expressed their determination to leave

The Exodus

their churches and manses. Several eyes were filled with tears. When the vanguard reached George Street they were received with cheers by a sympathetic crowd, and were constrained by them to fall into line. All the ministers who took part in that procession, and probably all the elders, have now passed from this earthly scene. A few students and other younger men who joined them are still spared.

Their new place of meeting was Tanfield Hall, Canonmills, on the north side of Edinburgh, fitted up hastily to accommodate three thousand persons. Like St. Andrew's Church, it had been filled early in the day. Among those present was the venerable Dr. John Brown of Broughton Place, an outspoken Voluntary. He had taken his place in the portion of the hall reserved for the members, thus unconsciously anticipating more than one event of later days, when Dr. James Buchanan of the High Church, Edinburgh, afterwards Professor, grasping his hand, exclaimed: "I am glad to see you here," Dr. Brown replied in the same words, emphasising the last one. Dr. Welsh, with his brother protesters, was received with enthusiasm. Engaging in prayer, as he had done in St. Andrew's Church, he, in a few sentences, proposed Dr. Chalmers as his successor. The motion was received with acclamation. The new Moderator again engaged in devotional exercises. The Psalm he selected was xliii. 3, to the end. When the lines, "Oh send Thy light forth and Thy truth" were sounded through the hall the sun burst out from a heavy thundercloud which had been concealing it, and shone brightly. A living historian, who can hardly be called favourable to the new Church, holds that no one can deny to her "the credit of a solemn, an enthusiastic, and a dignified opening scene." Speaking in the House of Commons, Mr. Gladstone (who was a subordinate member of Sir Robert Peel's ministry in 1843), as Prime Minister of England, spoke of her as "a body to whose moral attitude scarcely any word weaker or lower than

The Exodus

that of majesty is, according to the spirit of historical criticism, justly applicable."

The Assembly that met at Canonmills sat till Tuesday, May 30th, when it rose an hour after midnight. We cannot dwell upon its proceedings, the measures taken in regard to missions, support of the ministry, church building, etc., in order to carry on the work of the church in its new surroundings. Two things, however, must be noticed. The deputations that had been sent by the Irish and English Presbyterian Churches to the Church of Scotland laid their commissions on the table at Canonmills. The Original Secession Church also sent a deputation.

The other event to which we allude is the Signing of the Deed of Demission, which took place on Tuesday, 23rd May. This document contained the renunciation by the signatories of their status, privileges, and emoluments as ministers of the Establishment, reserving to themselves only their interest in the Widows' Fund. This incident has formed the subject of D. O. Hill's celebrated picture. He represents Dr. Chalmers in the chair as Moderator; Dr. Welsh, Ex-Moderator, on his right hand; Sir James Forrest, the Lord Provost of Edinburgh, on his left; Dr. Patrick Macfarlan of Greenock, the holder of the best parish living, adhibiting his name at the table; Dr. Candlish, with a paper in his hand, calling the roll. The members were called up, ten at a time, in the order of Presbyteries. The signing occupied most of the forenoon, and had to be resumed in the evening. The number of signatures, including subsequent additions, amount to four hundred and seventy-four, fully the third of the unbroken Church. All the Missionaries to the Jews, and those in the foreign field, except, we believe, one lady on the staff, adhered. We should further mention that nearly two hundred preachers, and a large body of divinity students, also joined the movement. The Deed was sent to the Assembly sitting at St. Andrew's Church. There the ministers who had signed it were declared to be no longer ministers of the Establishment, or entitled to receive a presentation. But they were not deposed. The Queen's letter had endorsed, if not emphasised, the decision of the Law Courts and the Legislature. It stated in substance that the Church, being established by statute, the Union was indissoluble while the statute remained unrepealed. The Assembly treated the Veto and Chapel Acts of 1834, and the deposition of the Strathbogie ministers, as null and void. A committee was appointed to answer the Protest. They were authorised to report to the August Commission. When that crowded body met, they received the Report but avoided discussing or approving of it, perhaps under Government influence, in order to prevent further division. The modern historian of the Church of Scotland writes thus of its condition in 1843: "The Church was left miserably weak, like a man bled within an ace of his death."

As the Episcopalians fell out of our review when we dealt with the Revolution Settlement, so now the Established

Church falls out. We have dealt with her only in connection with those who separated from time to time from her. We therefore do not propose to dwell on the Parliamentary Legislation of 1843-44. Nor shall we discuss the question of the Church's relation to the Claim of Right, which, though rejected by the Civil Power, is still on the records of her Assembly; the effect of the alteration in 1874 of the Patronage Law on the statutes of the Empire; or the cause of her growth in recent years.

CHAPTER VII.

THE FREE CHURCH—COMPARISON BETWEEN 1638-62 AND 1843.

THOSE who took part in the exodus of 1843 applied to it the designation of The Disruption, a designation that has almost universally been adopted. It indicates their position. They did not consider themselves Seceders. They intended to carry out the work of the Church independent of State connection. They therefore assumed the name of the Free Church of Scotland, a name that seems destined to have an interesting history. The word Free has been adopted within recent years by the Nonconformist bodies of England, and the name Free Church of Scotland has been appropriated by the minority which stood out against the Union of 1900. In 1843 a new ecclesiastical situation was created. Two churches claimed the allegiance of the nation. This invites comparison with the eras of the Covenant and those of the foundation of the Secession and Relief—between 1843 and 1638-62, between 1843, 1733, and 1752.

In 1843, 1638 and 1662 were in a sense combined. When, in 1638, the Royal Commissioner dissolved the Assembly, it continued to sit and deposed the bishops. The Church prospered, as we said at the outset, till it became divided into Resolutionists and Protesters. In 1662 the exodus consisted of one-third of the ministers, and these could not preach to their congregations or take ecclesiastical action. In 1843 those who formed the Free Church could, ere they left the Establishment, have raised a debate or forced a vote, and this might have made the conflict with the State more acute; but they adopted the more prudent course of withdrawing. Their ministrations continued. The Church Courts met. Notwithstanding the trials endured in leaving the manses, the difficulties in

The Free Church 105

obtaining sites for their buildings, and the friction that occurred in many cases between landlords and tenants, employers and employed, friends, and members of the same family, the work prospered. In both cases the proportion of the ministers was the same. In 1662 the ministers of Edinburgh and Glasgow, with one exception in each, left their churches. In 1843, the majority, not only in these two cities, but in most of the towns, joined the Free Church. In Brechin and Stirling, all, three in number, did so. In the rural districts there was a marked contrast. Where the one had been strong the other was comparatively weak. In the South and West of Scotland most of the ministers left in 1662. In 1843 this cannot be said to have been the case. In some Presbyteries there were only one or two. The highest proportion seems to have been in the Presbytery of Greenock, twelve out of sixteen adhering to the Free Church. In the Counties north of Aberdeen there were hardly a dozen that did not conform in 1662. In 1843 there were nearly one hundred, almost a fourth of those who signed the Deed of Demission. In the Presbytery of Tain, only one minister adhered to the Establishment. In several other cases only two or three did so. In the Synod of Ross there were only seven. In the Synod of Perth and Stirling about a half cast in their lot with the Free Church. In Argyll, Fife, and Angus and Mearns there were a third. In the three Presbyteries most closely associated with the Ten Years' Conflict, the numbers stood thus — Auchterarder and Dunkeld, seven each; Strathbogie, three ministers and the ordained missionaries that supplied the Parishes of those deposed. It is interesting to note that all the Secession ministers who joined the Church of Scotland in 1839, and were in it in 1843, adhered to the Free Church, except two — the Rev. William Dalziel, Dunfermline, who was presented to Thurso; and the Rev. William Elder, Cupar - Fife, who was translated to Tealing.

The Free Church

Both in 1662 and 1843 most of the ministers who withdrew from the Establishment were young men. In the latter year only twelve had been ordained in the XVIII century. Of these two died before they left their manses—Mr George Logan of Eastwood, the first father of the Free Church (bearing, strange to say, the same name as the Moderator who had pronounced sentence of deposition on the eight Seceders), in his eighty-fifth year and fifty-eighth of his ministry; and Dr. Thomas Ross of Lochbroom. Another of these, the Rev. Andrew Ferguson of Maryton, died the day after he left the house he had occupied for fifty-eight years. Most of the younger ministers were probably students of Dr. Chalmers. The surviving minister of the Secessionists of 1662 was the Rev. Thomas Warner of Balmaclellan, who returned to his Parish at the Revolution, and died father of the Church of Scotland, 1716, in the eighty-fifth year of his age, and fifty-ninth of his ministry. The only survivor of those of 1843 is the venerable Dr. Thomas Smith, now in his eighty-ninth year, and the sixty-seventh of his ministry, who has served her in the Foreign field, in the ministry at home, and also as a Professor. In the *Disruption Annals*, the number of Disruption ministers, including missionaries, is given as five hundred and two. It will be remembered that not all the supporters of Non-Intrusion, nor all those who signed the Convocation Resolutions, left the Establishment. Of the bulk of the men of 1662 little is known, beyond the fact that they were men of piety and ability. Those of 1843 were also fully up to that average. As a class they influenced the religious life of Scotland, and through it the general life of the nation for at least a generation. The effects of their influence are still felt, and will tell for many years to come, in our towns and rural districts. We may therefore subject the list to a little examination.

Seven who had occupied the Moderator's Chair in the undivided Church, including Dr. Patrick Macfarlan of

Greenock, who held the wealthiest living in Scotland, were among the number. For fifty years (with one exception, 1887, when Principal Rainy was Moderator), the Chair of the Free Assembly was filled by men ordained before 1843, men of scholarship, piety and Christian character selected from various parts of the country. Others of equal standing declined the honour when offered to them. Besides Drs. Chalmers and Welsh, two professors left the universities and occupied chairs in the New College, Edinburgh,—Dr. Alexander Black, Professor of Divinity in Marischal College, Aberdeen, and the Rev. Dr. John Fleming, Professor of Natural Philosophy in King's College, in the same city. Fifteen other Disruption ministers, elected to conduct the classes in the Divinity Halls at Edinburgh, Glasgow, and Aberdeen, included such men as William Cunningham, James Bannerman, George Smeaton, Patrick Fairbairn, and David Brown, all well known as theological writers. At least one hundred and twenty of the ministers had the degree of Doctor of Divinity. Many were notable preachers in their own districts, where their memory will long be cherished. Some of these were translated from country to town charges, hardly to the advantage of the Church in rural districts. Among the preachers may be named Drs. Candlish, Guthrie, John Bruce, C. J. Brown and Moody Stuart, of Edinburgh; Buchanan, Somerville, and Arnot, of Glasgow; Davidson of Aberdeen; M'Donald of Blairgowrie, latterly of North Leith; and Cooper of Burntisland. In the Highlands there were Dr. M'Donald, Urquhart, known as the "Apostle of the North," and many others. Among missionaries we single out the apostolic Alexander Duff of Calcutta, the scholarly John Wilson of Bombay, J. Ross of Pirie, South Africa, and the learned Dr. John Duncan, well known as Rabbi Duncan, of the Jewish Mission at Buda-Pesth. Several went to other lands. Dr. William Chalmers of Dailly became Principal of the Presbyterian College, London; Dr. James

M'Cosh of Brechin, a well-known philosophical writer, Principal of Princeton, U.S.A. Dr. Stewart of Erskine became known as "of Leghorn"; Dr. James Lewis of Leith, as "of Rome." Among those who founded or strengthened Colonial churches were Thomas Burns of Monckton, the nephew of the national poet, who went to Otago, New Zealand; Drs. Adam Cairns, Cupar, to Melbourne, Australia; Robert Burns, Paisley, George M'Leod, Logie Easter, and Alexander Topp, Elgin, to North America. Many of the Disruption ministers were authors, publishing volumes of sermons, single discourses, and pamphlets. Amongst biblical and religious writers were the cultured Drs. Tweedie of Edinburgh, Lorimer of Glasgow, Keith of St. Cyrus (the writer on Prophecy), Foote of Brechin, A. S. Paterson of Glasgow, and Blaikie of Drumblade, afterwards Professor. Drs. Landsborough of Stevenston and Longmuir of Aberdeen were well-known as skilled in science, Drs. Hetherington of Torphichen, afterwards Professor; M'Lauchlan of Moy, afterwards of Edinburgh, and James M'Kenzie, Dalbeattie, afterwards of Dunfermline, are well-known historians. Other writers who may be singled out are Dr. Hanna of Skirling (the only minister in the South of Scotland whose entire congregation, with a single exception, left the Establishment along with him), afterwards of St. John's, Edinburgh, the biographer of his father-in-law, Dr. Chalmers, and author of six volumes on our Lord's Life on Earth, and other works; Andrew Bonar of Collace, author of the biography of M'Cheyne and other works, and his brother, Horatius Bonar of Kelso, the poet and hymnist. It may be interesting to our readers if we note a few facts of a more personal nature. One Disruption minister, the Rev. Henry Moncreiff of East Kilbride, succeeded to a baronetcy. Five, the Rev. James Begg of Liberton, afterwards Dr. Begg of Edinburgh; the Rev. Thomas M'Lauchlan of Moy, afterwards Dr. M'Lauchlan of Edinburgh; his brother Simon, of Cawdor; the Rev. Thomas Jolly of Bowden, and

The Free Church

the Rev. William Ferrie, Anstruther Easter, withdrew from the Establishment, whilst their fathers remained Parish ministers,—the Rev. James Begg of New Monkland, the Rev. James M'Lauchlan of Moy, to whom his son had been colleague, the Rev. Thomas Jolly of Dunnet, and Dr. William Ferrie, Kilconquhar, Professor of Civil History, St. Andrews. Dr. William Thomson of Perth, and the Rev. John Thomson of Shettleston, Glasgow, latterly of Aberdeen, the brother and half-brother of the celebrated Dr. Andrew Thomson, each lived to be father of the Free Church. Dr. William Thomson's son, the Rev. John Thomson of Moneydie, was also a Disruption minister. There were four instances of fathers and sons being colleagues—the Ingrams of Unst, Keiths of St. Cyrus, Kennedys of Dornoch, and Mackenzies of Tongue. The story of the last pair is pathetic. The older one had been colleague to his own father. Thus father and son had been born in the same manse. When they left in 1843 they found accommodation in the end of the parish schoolmaster's house, the ladies of the family retiring to Thurso, forty miles distant. The father took bronchitis and the son bilious fever, and they died within a month of each other, in the summer of 1845, one in his seventy-fifth year, the other in his thirtieth. There were two cases of a father and two sons; Dr. Henry Duncan of Ruthwell, the founder of Savings Banks and author of *Sacred Philosophy of the Seasons* and other works, with George John of Kirkpatrick-Durham, who eventually settled in England, and William Wallace of Cleish, afterwards of Peebles; and Dr. Hugh Laird, a successor of Ebenezer Erskine at Portmoak, with Alexander of Abbotshall, afterwards of Dundee, and Dr. John of Inverkeillor, latterly of Cupar-Fife, Moderator in 1889. We note six instances of father and son, Drs. Lorimer of Haddington and of Glasgow; Browns of Langton and of Kinneff, the latter afterwards of Edinburgh, editor of the *Disruption Annals*, and Moderator in

The Free Church

1890; the Rev. James Miller of Monikie, and Dr. Samuel of Monifieth and Glasgow; the Carments of Rosskeen and Comrie; the Inneses of Deskford and Seafield, Cullen, afterwards of Canonbie; and Macgillivrays of Lairg and Dairsie. There were two groups of three brothers, Drs. William Burns of Kilsyth, father of the church, Robert of Paisley, afterwards of Canada, and George of Tweedsmuir, latterly of Corstorphine; and Drs. J. J. Bonar of Greenock, Horatius of Kelso, latterly of Edinburgh, and Andrew of Collace and Glasgow, the last two, Moderators in 1883 and in 1878 respectively. Other two brothers filled the Moderator's Chair, Dr. Charles Brown of Edinburgh in 1872 and Dr. David of Ord, afterwards of Glasgow, and Principal at Aberdeen, Moderator in 1885. There were also five other pairs of brothers, Dr. Nathaniel Paterson of Glasgow, author of the *Manse Garden* and Moderator in 1850, and Walter of Kirkurd; James Lewis of Leith and Rome, and George of Dundee and Ormiston; Messrs. Anderson of Kippen and Blantyre; Dr. Patrick Fairbairn of Saltoun, afterwards Principal of the Glasgow College, Moderator in 1864, and John of Greenlaw; the Bannatynes of Old Cumnock and of Oban, afterwards of Glasgow. One of the Calcutta missionaries was the Rev. John M'Donald, the son of the Apostle of the North. Dr. Ingram of Unst died in his one hundred and third year, the oldest minister in Scotland. None of those ministers who are reckoned as leaders of the Free Church lived to an advanced age. Dr. Welsh died in his fifty-second year, Dr. Cunningham in his fifty-ninth, Dr. Guthrie in his seventieth, Dr. Robert Buchanan in his seventy-third, Drs. Chalmers and Candlish in their sixty-eighth, the life of the latter being a few months longer than that of the former. These last two died at the same age as Ralph Erskine.

The evening before he died, Dr. Chalmers had said. "I expect to give worship to-morrow morning," and retired to rest apparently in his usual health. In the morning the housekeeper knocked at the door of his room and receiving no answer entered, opened the shutters and withdrew the curtains. She found him half erect, his head reclining gently on the pillow. There had been no pain or struggle, his ransomed spirit had passed from earth and joined the white-robed multitude in their heavenly worship of the Lamb upon the throne. His death occurred in the night of the Lord's Day, 30th May 1847, or early on the following morning. The General Assembly was sitting. It adjourned till after the funeral, thus prolonging its sittings for about a week. The funeral was one of the largest seen in Edinburgh. The procession contained the Magistrates and Town Council in their robes, members of the General Assembly, other ministers and officebearers of the Church, professors, probationers and students, ministers of other denominations, and a large number of the public, the officers of the Assembly and professors wearing their gowns and bands, all marching four abreast. It was witnessed by a multitude estimated at about one hundred thousand. The place of interment was the Grange Cemetery, where the mortal remains of many loyal Free Churchmen have since been laid. The whole was a tribute to the high character of Thomas Chalmers, the founder of the fourth section of the United Free Church. A writer in the *Witness* newspaper says: "There was a moral sublimity in the spectacle. It spoke more emphatically than by words of the dignity of intrinsic excellence and of the height to which a true man may attain. It was the dust of a Presbyterian minister which the coffin contained, and yet they were burying him amid the tears of a nation and with more than kingly honours." The memory of the large-hearted and catholic-minded Chalmers lives in all sections of the Church of Christ.

It will be remembered that Chalmers and the other ecclesiastical leaders of the Disruption movement were ably supported by laymen in every rank of life. In addition to those already referred to, we may single out among peers the Marquis of Breadalbane; landed proprietors, David Maitland Macgill Crichton, Esq. of Rankeillour, connected with the Lauderdale family, and Alexander Campbell, Esq. of Monzie; among lawyers, Sheriffs Graham Speirs of Midlothian and Alexander Earle Monteith of Fifeshire. We might add many more, but we must specially allude to one whose writings influenced the masses. We, of course, mean Hugh Miller, the stonemason of Cromarty, one of the pioneers of the science of geology in Scotland, and a master of English prose, author of *My Schools and Schoolmasters; The Testimony of the Rocks*, and other works. A patriotic Scotsman, he, after the decision of the House of Lords in the Auchterarder case, addressed his well known letter on that case to Lord Brougham. In the following year, 1840, he was offered by the Non-Intrusion leaders the editorship of the *Witness*. That powerful and ably-conducted paper was devoted to the rights of the people in Church matters, Spiritual Independence and Evangelical religion. Its articles produced a deep impression and greatly aided the cause it supported. It has been claimed for Hugh Miller that the cause of the Free Church at its commencement owes more to him than to any other man, Chalmers alone excepted.

CHAPTER VIII.

THE FREE CHURCH—COMPARISON AND CONTRAST, 1681, 1733, 1752,—1843.

WHEN we compare the Movement of 1843 and the earlier Separations, we find a contrast, and also a similarity, with a difference. The Reformed Presbyterian, the Secession, and the Relief Churches, as we have seen, sprang from small beginnings, and grew gradually, preserving evangelical teaching in our towns and remote rural parishes, but were restricted to certain districts. As the Reformed Presbyterian Church had prepared the way for the Secession and the Relief, so all these three may be said to have sown the seed, and the Free Church reaped her share of the harvest. A few of the ministers, and doubtless a proportion of the people, had originally belonged to the older sections of what is now the United Free Church.

The Free Church, on the other hand, commenced with most of the appliances necessary for advancing the work of the Church. These were speedily utilised. All over Scotland congregations were formed; churches and manses and other ecclesiastical buildings erected; schools and divinity halls opened; home, foreign, and colonial missions carried on. The success achieved might almost be called phenomenal. Dr. Bryce, the Established Church historian of the Ten Years' Conflict, in his almost forgotten but curious and not uninteresting book, describes it thus: "Time must tell how far all these gigantic exertions are to prove effectual in sustaining a fabric which, as it was reared with almost miraculous rapidity, it may be expected will fall with equal celerity. After the lapse of three years from the secession, the Free Church could boast of eight hundred and sixteen congregations, six hundred and sixty-two ministers, two hundred thousand communicants, six hun-

The Free Church

dred churches, and one hundred and seventy-one manses. The pecuniary resources to sustain this machinery in full efficiency had amounted, during these three years, to one million, one hundred and forty thousand pounds, sterling, of which there only remained one hundred and fifty thousand pounds unpaid up." Dr. Bryce's anticipations of collapse have not been realised. But, of course, success has not advanced in the same ratio as during the first three years. We do not propose to enter into the details of the history of that success. The Free Church has provoked other Churches, both in Great Britain and other lands, to good works. During the last sixty years, a large spirit of liberality has been created. Church extension has been carried on in Scotland, especially in the cities and in the mining districts, where the population has so enormously increased. The cause of Foreign Missions has been advanced in almost every land. Many ministers have gone forth to minister to their fellow-countrymen in the Colonies.

The Divinity Halls of the Free Church were more fully equipped than any others ever have been in Scotland. Some of the Professors have had almost world-wide reputation. Not to speak of those already referred to, or to those yet spared, we may mention of the second generation the late A. B. Davidson of Edinburgh, A. B. Bruce and James Candlish of Glasgow, and W. Robertson Smith of Aberdeen.

We now turn to the similarity. At its formation, the Secession Church, as we have seen, did not join with the Reformed Presbyterian, nor did the Relief join with either. The Free Church joined with none of the three. One reason for this is stated plainly by Dr. Chalmers in his opening address as Moderator in 1843: "The Voluntaries mistake us if they consider us to be Voluntaries. . . . Though we quit the Establishment, we go out on the Establishment principle; we quit a vitiated Establishment. but would rejoice in returning to a pure one. To express it otherwise, we are the advocates for a national recognition and national support of religion, and we are not Voluntaries." The Reformed Presbyterians from the beginning adhered to the Covenant. The Seceders, not satisfied with holding their own views of the Revolution Settlement, renewed the Covenants, although, as we have seen, they eventually dropped them. The Relief alone kept itself disentangled. The Free Church rested its historical basis on the Claim of Right, its own interpretation of the Revolution Settlement. That Church never issued a Testimony. The only Act that approaches it in character is a Declaration by the Assembly of 1851, which was not sent down to Presbyteries for approval, but was prefixed to a volume entitled, *The Subordinate Standards and other authoritative documents of the Free Church of Scotland*, published by the authority of the General Assembly. The Cameronians and the Seceders had required adherence to the Covenants from their office-bearers, and to some extent from their members. No approval of the Claim of Right was required by the Free Church from her members. The relation of office-bearers to that document was defined in the Formula signed by and Questions put to them at Ordination and Admission. The Formula and Questions were drawn up by Drs. Cunningham and Candlish, approved of by the majority of Presbyteries, and passed by the Assembly of 1846. In the preamble it is stated that the Church does not regard anything in the Confession as favouring intolerance or persecution. Probationers and all office-bearers are required at license, ordination, or admission to office, to approve of "the general principles embodied in the Claim . . . with respect to the spirituality and freedom of the Church of Christ and her subjection to Him as her only Head, and to His Word as her only standard." Ministers were further required to disown Erastian tenets. Principal Cunningham explained to his students that there was no desire to bind the ministers to any interpretation of the

The Free Church

historical facts embodied in the Claim. These facts are referred to in support of the 1843 view of State Connection. Thus no one seems bound to the Revolution Settlement, or even, perhaps, to State connection. The position, though probably unavoidable in the middle of the XIX century, looks somewhat inconsistent. The Church, as a whole, appears to be bound to the Claim; no individual office-bearer seems to be so. There may be in all this no opinion expressed, or even implied, regarding Creed first and Church second, or Church first and Creed second. But it is again Spiritual Independence first, State Connection second. It leaves the door open for later developments.

CHAPTER IX.

THE UNITED PRESBYTERIAN CHURCH; 1847.

WE have lingered perhaps unnecessarily over the story of Separation. We now turn to what, if it be not so full of striking incident, is more pleasant and congenial, the story of Union. On the cover of the *Missionary Record* there are three Union dates. We insert another, which stands second, the Union of the Original Secession with the Free Church. The four are 1847, 1852. 1876, 1900.

The first of these, if not so well remembered in the last and present generation as 1843, a year of separation, occupies a prominent place in the ecclesiastical and religious history of Scotland. It marks the turning of the tide. It witnessed the union of the Secession and Relief Churches, which formed the United

Presbyterian Church, the Union which may be pre-eminently entitled the Happy Union. The uniting parties had separated from the Establishment, as we have already seen, in circumstances slightly different, but on grounds similar or, rather, identical. They had not united, but had occupied positions far apart from each other, the one, to use the language of our day, narrow, the other broad. The one adhered to the Covenants, the other kept itself disentangled from all historical documents; the one was strict in its terms of communion, the other liberal. The wonder, perhaps, is that they united at all. But we, living in the XX century, looking back, see that this Union was only a matter of time. It came very gradually. The stricter party sat looser and looser to historical documents, and their terms of communion were slowly relaxed. It would appear that the attention of the smaller Synod was first directed to this matter in a resolution it minuted shortly after the re-union of the Burghers and Anti-Burghers. No other steps were taken till 1834, the same year in which the Veto Law was passed, and one year after the centenary of the Secession. The prime mover was a young minister, the Rev. William Mackelvie, afterwards the Annalist of the United Presbyterian Church, and its Moderator in 1856. His church at Balgedie was situated in Ebenezer Erskine's first parish, Portmoak, not far from Gairney Bridge. In his own Presbytery he proposed an overture to the Synod to take steps to maintain friendly relations with the Relief Synod. He suggested to two ministers of that Synod to propose, in their own Presbytery (the one within whose bounds the first Presbytery of Relief was founded), an overture in similar terms. The negotiations then begun extended over thirteen years. They were hindered by the excitement in the country owing to the Non-Intrusion and Church Extension movements, by the formation of the Free Church, by the well-known Campbeltown case (a case in the Civil Courts about Church property within the Relief Synod).

and by the Atonement controversy in the Secession Church. It is unnecessary to linger over details, resolutions of Synods, and reports of committees. The basis of Union was finally agreed upon at a meeting of each Synod held simultaneously in October 1846. It was there resolved that the solemn and interesting event should take place in the May following, one hundred years and one month after the breach of the Burghers and Anti-Burghers. It was decided that the meeting should be held in Bristo Church, Edinburgh. the scene of the Breach and re-union. But the building was found to be too small. Tanfield Hall, offered by the officials of the Free Church, was eventually selected. This building was thus the cradle of both the Free and the United Presbyterian Churches. Commenting upon this in his narrative of the Union, prepared at the request of the Synod, Dr. Mackelvie writes: "What the intention of Providence is in thus overruling so many minds, and constraining them to a reluctant choice, time must develop; we put the coincidences upon record with the view of assisting the interpreter of events to read the mind of God in them. Meanwhile Tanfield Hall has become a place of historical association, and it is no disparagement to it that the United Presbyterian Church has helped to make it so. A public journal referring to this fact, beautifully remarked that 'The Disruption' and 'The Union' meetings which took place there were both events for good, but the one was like the bursting of a torrent, the other was like the meeting of the waters." The Synods met on the same day, 10th May 1847, the larger in Broughton Place, the smaller in St. James's Place. When the minutes of the former Synods were read, there was unanimity in the Secession, but in the Relief there were two dissentients. (One of these brethren, Dr. John Craig of Cupar, afterwards joined the Established Church, and died in his manse at Sandwick in Shetland, nearly fifty years later, aged ninety-three.) On the 13th the Synods marched from their places of meet-

United Presbyterian Church

ing three abreast; the larger one in order of seniority, ministers of thirty years standing first, then those over twenty, then over ten, then younger; the smaller one in order of Presbyteries. In the hall they took their seats in such a manner as enabled them to give each other the right hand of fellowship. Tanfield was again filled from floor to ceiling. The Moderators took their places on either side of the vacant chair reserved for the Moderator of the United Synod. Mr. Auld, the Moderator of the Relief Synod, began the proceedings by giving out Psalm cxxxiii. After the preliminaries, including the reading of the minutes of the Synods and the basis of Union, the Moderators, the Revs. William Auld of Greenock, and John (afterwards Dr.) Newlands of Perth, declared in similar terms the two churches to be one, and gave each other the right hand of fellowship. The ministers present followed their example, amid the acclamations of the spectators. Thereafter Mr. Auld nominated as first Moderator of the United Synod, Dr. William Kidston, of

East Campbell Street, Glasgow, formerly Secession, the oldest minister present, then in his eightieth year, and for nearly fifty-seven years a minister. On taking the chair, Dr. Kidston read Psalm cxxxii., constituted the Synod by prayer, and then gave out the first three verses of Psalm cxlvii., which had been sung at the Union of the Burghers and Anti - Burghers. Devotional exercises were then engaged in, and addresses delivered by Professors Lindsay and Harper.

In the evening a soiree was held in Tanfield, which was packed to the utmost, so that there had to be an overflow meeting, attended by about a thousand persons. Over the larger meeting, one of the founders of the Evangelical Alliance, the large-hearted and liberal-handed friend of missions, John Henderson, Esq. of Park, presided; over the smaller, a son of the Secession manse, James Peddie, W.S., the indefatigable Treasurer of the Synod. The speakers, with the exception of Dr. Bryce, of the Associate Presbytery of Ireland, were selected from the uniting churches. Among these were Dr. Gavin Struthers, the historian of the Relief Church, and well-known preachers, such as Dr. William Anderson and Dr. David King of Glasgow. In reading these speeches some time ago, we found that the views expressed on the connection between Church and State were more pronounced and extreme than those held at the present day.

Thus the Secession Church (after an existence of nearly one hundred and fourteen years from the meeting at Gairney Bridge, and twenty-seven from the Union of the Burghers and Anti-Burghers) and the Relief (ninety-five years after the deposition of Gillespie, and eighty-six after the formation of the first Presbytery) finished their separate histories, and were merged in the United Presbyterian Church. The position of the ministers was now in every sense improved. The Church at once took its place side by side with the Established and Free Churches. There were now three great Presbyterian Churches in Scotland. The youngest one made its influence felt in all questions relating to the religious, ecclesiastical, moral, social, and educational interests of the country, especially in temperance reform, and the religious instruction of the young.

The Union comprised 518 congregations: 400 Secession, of which 56 were in England; 118 Relief, 4 in England. There were also, in connection with the Secession, missionaries labouring in Jamaica and in Old Calabar, West Africa. Among the ministers were Professors John Brown, Harper, M'Michael, Lindsay, and the well-known commentator, the catholic-minded John Eadie; and among the younger men the learned John Cairns, afterwards Professor and Principal, and the accomplished preacher John Ker: not to mention others, esteemed for their pulpit power and as writers in various departments of literature. We need not name those who, ordained after the Union, attained to eminence, and have passed to their rest and reward. Only three ministers whose names stand on the roll of the first Synod are now living. Two belonged to the Relief, Dr.

Robert Frew, St. Ninians, now the oldest surviving minister in Scotland, ordained 1835, and the Rev. David Anderson, Ceres, who dissented from, but adhered to, the Union, 1840. The third is the Rev. John B. Ritchie, Charlotte Street, Aberdeen, United Secession, 1845. The United Presbyterian Church engaged in Church extension in our larger cities and in England. The Associate Presbytery of Ireland was received into it in 1858. It became pre-eminently a Missionary Church, taking a high place in this respect among the churches of Britain. Its agents were found in the West Indies, Western and Southern Africa, India, China and Japan.

The basis of Union need not detain us long. It consists of ten articles. The office-bearers at their admission were asked to approve of them. The Larger and Shorter Catechisms are recognised, along with the Westminster Confession, as the standards, it being declared that there is no approval of persecuting or intolerant principles in religion. There is an article stating that the election of office-bearers belongs exclusively to members in full communion, and another enjoining on all the duty of supporting ordinances by voluntary contributions. All direct reference to the Covenants or historical documents of any kind is omitted, the right of private judgment is reserved regarding the proceedings of our forefathers, and the causes of separation from the Establishment are still held valid. Thus the question of State connection is left at least an open one. The question of Creed first, Church second, or Church first, Creed second, does not appear to have been prominently before the mind of the framers of the basis of Union. Spiritual Independence was again first, State relation subordinate; we should perhaps say very subordinate. Regarding free Communion, as understood by the Relief, all had the right of acting on their conscientious convictions. It would seem that in the United Church, of 1847, the principles of the smaller Church, the more large-hearted one of Gillespie and his followers, prevailed along the whole line.

CHAPTER X.

THE ORIGINAL SECEDERS—UNION WITH THE FREE CHURCH, 1852.

THE next union, that of the Original Seceders and the Free Church was of a different complexion. We have already seen that the minority of the Old Light Burghers, who refused to join the Establishment in 1839, had united with the Old Light Anti-Burghers, the M'Crieites, as they were popularly called, from the biographer of Knox having belonged to them. That union took place on the 18th May 1842, exactly one year before the Disruption. On the following day the Synod of the United Original Secession Church renewed the Covenant, which was signed by thirty ministers, one missionary, seven probationers, six students and thirty-three ruling elders. One minister of the

Burgher section, the Rev. John M'Kinlay of Renton, stood out against the Union and joined the Reformed Presbyterians. Two ministers of the Anti-Burgher section also stood out, the Rev. James Wright of Edinburgh, and the Rev. Andrew Lambie, Pitcairngreen. These two (the Two Witnesses, as they were sometimes called) afterwards parted company. The Original Seceders sympathised with the Free Church from 1843. Committees were appointed by both parties with a view to union, but negotiations were dropped. The Seceders about the same time entered into similar negotiations with the Reformed Presbyterians, but these were also dropped. The adoption by the Assembly of 1851 of the Act and Declaration now prefixed to the "Subordinate Standards of the Free Church," led to a renewal of the Union movement among the Seceders. The proposal for union was brought forward by an overture, signed by nineteen ministers, in the Synod held April 1852. After an able and keen debate, extending over two days, it was adopted by a majority of one; eighteen ministers and fourteen elders voting for it, thirteen ministers and eighteen elders against it. The Moderator and five ministers who did not take part in the vote were in favour of it. It is curious to note that the mover of the amendment against Union, the Rev. James Anderson of Carluke, had originally been an Old Light Burgher and the mover of the amendment against the Union of 1839 with the Establishment. The argument for union practically was that its supporters considered themselves the legitimate representatives of the Erskines, recognised the Free Church as the Church of Scotland from which their ecclesiastical forefathers had seceded, and looked upon its General Assembly as the reforming one to which they should return. The objections to it were that the Free Church had not reached the attainment of the Second Reformation, and did not hold the binding obligations of the Covenants. A deputation appeared before the Assembly of 1852 on the evening of the second day of its sitting. The Free Church received the Seceders on their own standing, recognising their right to hold their own opinions regarding the action of the Erskines and the binding obligations of the Covenants. At the same time the Assembly, although some of its members were favourable to covenanting, pronounced no judgment on the subject. The Union was consummated on the last evening of the Assembly—the 1st of June. Again Tanfield was filled from floor to ceiling. Speeches were delivered by Drs. Candlish and Duff, Sir George Sinclair and Mr. Murray Dunlop, and the representatives of the Seceders received the right hand of fellowship from the Moderator, the venerable and gentlemanly Dr. Angus Mackellar. Three of the deputation, the younger Thomas M'Crie, their Moderator; Dr. Shaw, Whitburn, the clerk of the Synod; and the Rev. William White, Haddington, editor of their magazine addressed the Assembly. Those who listened to the thrilling addresses of Drs. Candlish and

The Original Seceders 143

Duff can never forget the effect they produced. When read more than fifty years after delivery, these speeches have an old-fashioned sound, a sound unfamiliar not only to our younger members, but also to our younger ministers. For the moment, the uniting parties appeared to have overlooked the fact that there were other Presbyterian churches in the country besides themselves. The Free Church was recognised as the Church of Scotland, not only of the Revolution, but of the first and second Reformations, standing midway between Erastianism and Voluntaryism. The sentences pronounced against the Erskines were repudiated. In the words of Mr. White of Haddington: " I believe that Knox, and Melville, and Henderson, if they had been alive in the days of the Erskines, would have become Seceders; and I believe that Ebenezer Erskine and William Wilson, if they had been living, would this evening have ceased to be Seceders by joining the Free Church of Scotland." This Union, like the Separations, placed Spiritual Independence first, State connection second, the Revolution Settlement third. The Assembly certainly endorsed the principles of the Erskines, which, if given effect to in the XVIII century, might have come into collision with the Revolution Settlement and the Treaty of Union between England and Scotland. This Union was a testimony to the position of the Free Church. The addition was not great—twenty-five congregations in all, three or four of which lost their property by entering into the Union. Among the ministers were several men of mark in their day. Besides those already mentioned, we might name Dr. James Wylie, Moderator of the Anti-Burgher Secession Synod at its Union with the Burghers in 1842, the author of the *History of Protestantism*, a history of Scotland, and several volumes on Popery and Prophecy; James Anderson, author of *The Martyrs of the Bass* and *The Ladies of the Reformation and of the Covenant;* James Young, biographer of John Welsh of

The Original Seceders

Ayr; Edward Thomson of Dundee, afterwards of Edinburgh, and James Black of Kirkcaldy. We should add that the Synod appointed a committee to meet with those who did not join the Free Church, to arrange about the disposal of the property, thus following to a certain extent the example set at the Union of the Burgher Seceders with the Church of Scotland in 1839. The representatives of the minority still exist under the designation of the Synod of the United Original Seceders, and adhere to the covenanting Reformation. They consist of twenty-six congregations in Scotland, scattered over the whole country from the Orkney Islands to Galloway, and two in Ireland, and they carry on a mission in India. It is perhaps worthy of note that all the Seceding ministers, those who joined the Free Church in 1852 and those who remained apart, have entered into their rest.

CHAPTER XI.

NEGOTIATIONS FOR UNION, 1853-1876.

The next date on the cover of the *Missionary Record* is 1876, the year of the Union of the Reformed Presbyterians with the Free Church. That movement was the outcome of a larger one—the ten years' negotiations between the United Presbyterians and the Free Church—a movement that requires more than a passing notice. In 1853 an overture from the Presbytery of Selkirk was laid on the table of the Free Assembly, the object of which was to induce that Court to bring the Claim of Right before the Government and the Legislature. One motive for this was that the Earl of Aberdeen, the Lord Aberdeen of the Disruption days, was now Prime Minister, and among his colleagues were Sir James

Graham, the author of the Queen's letter sent to the Assembly of 1843, Mr. Gladstone, and other followers of Sir Robert Peel. The Assembly did not sustain the overture, but appointed a committee on the Principles of the Church, which issued a series of tracts, historical and explanatory of the Church's principles. From 1853 to 1900 the Free Church abstained from again placing the Claim of Right before Parliament. The truth must be admitted that, although the leaders remained loyal to the principles of 1843, standing as they did half-way between Erastianism and Voluntaryism, they altered their standpoint on the question of State connection. There passed over them, perhaps semi-consciously, certainly imperceptibly and very gradually, but not unnaturally, a change which some years earlier might have been described as approaching to New Light views. This can easily be proved from their public utterances. Certainly it is evident the Church advanced on that question much more rapidly than the successors of the Erskines. We may merely allude in passing to the Cardross case, which arose about this time. By it the Spiritual Independence of the Church appeared to be endangered; but we need not dwell on it, as, on account of the turn it finally took, the position of the Church was not directly affected.

The first public movement towards union was made by Sir George Sinclair of Ulbster, the son of the compiler of the first Statistical Account of Scotland. Sir George had joined the Free Church in 1851, eight years after the Disruption. He issued, in 1857, a declaration signed by nearly one hundred and fifty laymen, almost equally divided between Free Churchmen and United Presbyterians. Among them were three Peers of the Realm—Breadalbane, Kintore, and Panmure, and Mr. Murray Dunlop, the author of the Claim of Right. When the proposal came before the Assembly, its consideration was passed from. Six years later this premature movement was followed by a larger one, which was intended to embrace the non-Established

Negotiations for Union 149

Presbyterian Churches of Scotland and England. The Free, United Presbyterian, and Reformed Presbyterian Churches entered into negotiations. Among the causes that contributed to this movement were the Revival of 1859-60, and the unions of Presbyterian Churches in the Colonies. It certainly received an impetus from the great speech by Principal William Cunningham (the last which he delivered) in 1862 on the Australian Union, when he said he could sign the United Presbyterian formula.

In May 1863 the United Presbyterian Synod met as usual about a fortnight before the Free Assembly. There, therefore, the question was first brought forward. Four overtures were tabled, one from an individual minister, one from the Kirk-Session of Broughton Place, Edinburgh, the remaining two from Presbyteries, both English, Lancaster and Berwick. that from the latter drawn up by Dr. John Cairns. The Synod agreed to appoint a committee to confer with similar com-

Eligibility was proposed. Opposition was again manifested, and a secession threatened. Certainly arrangements were made with the view of giving effect to the latter object. On Wednesday, the 28th May, the subject was discussed. The debate lasted seven hours, occupying the whole forenoon. In the evening Principal Candlish introduced an alteration in his motion which satisfied the other side. It has been generally understood that it was largely owing to the efforts of Dr. Thomas Smith, now the survivor of the Disruption band, that this was effected. Before the close of the Assembly there was engrossed in the minutes a document signed by four hundred and four ministers and elders: in this they recognised the hand of God in the progress of the Union movement, and stated that the prosecution of it was "a duty of deep and abiding obligation." Thus the Union negotiations were suspended, and Mutual Eligibility became the law of both churches. Ministers of the one church could now be called by congrega-

Negotiations for Union 153

tions in the other. The United Presbyterian Synod put on their record, "That the agreement brought out between the negotiating churches laid an adequate foundation in principle for their incorporating union, and furnished, with the circumstances in Providence, a strong call to it." We must give, all Christian men must give expression to admiration of the spirit that was manifested by the Synod. They acted like Christian men and Christian ministers, in the spirit of Him whose servants they are, "Who when He was reviled, reviled not again."

The negotiations were not without good results. Each church understood better the position of the other, and, indeed, its own position. Extreme Voluntaryism was on the one hand toned down. On the other, advance was made to broader views on the question of the responsibilities of the Civil Magistrate to Religion and the Church.

Another outcome was found in two unions, one in England the other in Scotland, both taking place in 1876. The

United Presbyterian Church had about one hundred congregations in England in five Presbyteries. These were formed into an English Synod under the Scottish one in 1863. With a membership of fully twenty thousand they were united in 1876 with the Presbyterian Church in England. The United Church assumed the name of the Presbyterian Church of England. To-day this Church is gradually extending its influence in every direction, and is carrying on successfully missionary operations, especially in China. The United Presbyterian Church thus sacrificed, for the sake of union, somewhere about a sixth of her congregations. The second resulting union will be dealt with in the following chapter.

CHAPTER XII.

THE REFORMED PRESBYTERIANS—UNION WITH THE FREE CHURCH, 1876.

THE other union to which we referred at the opening and close of the preceding chapter was that of the Reformed Presbyterian Church with the Free Church. This brings us back to the oldest portion of the United Free Church. We have already traced briefly her origin and history. In 1863 she had forty-six congregations with thirty-eight ministers and three missionaries, Messrs. Inglis, Paton and Copeland. The Professors were the younger Goold and Dr. Binnie of Stirling. The former became a Moderator, the latter a Professor of the Free Church. Dr. Goold was their leading man, devout, cultured, genial, a man of business, beloved by all, known throughout Scotland as the Secretary of the Eastern Section of the

National Bible Society. The year 1863 was an eventful one in the history of the Reformed Presbyterian Synod. It was a year of Secession or Separation. The point in dispute was again the relation of the Church to the Civil Government. After the passing of the first Reform Bill, the Synod had declared that the exercise of the Franchise was "inconsistent with the privileges of the Church." This decision was to a certain extent disregarded. There was no uniform practice among the Kirk-Sessions regarding the application of discipline. The question was discussed at several meetings of Synod. It was referred to a committee. The final decision was given in 1863. That practically was a recommendation to the members to abstain from the use of the Franchise, and from taking the Oath of Allegiance, and an enactment that "discipline to the effect of suspension and expulsion from the Church should cease." This was carried by 46 to 11. Thereafter Mr. Anderson, Loanhead, protested, and claimed all the rights of the Reformed Presbyterian Church. He and

The Reformed Presbyterians 157

three other ministers, with elders and members of other congregations, formed another Synod. The majority did not formally cut off and depose the minority, and they soon recovered the loss. The members of the minority have all passed into the unseen world, including the youngest, the Rev. Robert Martin of Wishaw, editor of the Sermons of Alexander Henderson, and a young man of great promise. The Synod still exists. It consists of eleven congregations, and has missions in Antioch and Alexandria. It retains its attitude of passive opposition to the present form of the Civil Government of the country. It binds itself or holds itself bound to the Covenants and historical documents of the XVII century. This Separation of 1863 had nothing to do with the Union with the Free Church.

That year, as we have seen, was the one in which the negotiations for Union between the Free and United Presbyterian Churches were opened. These Churches invited the Original Seceders and Reformed Presbyterians to join them. The former declined on account of their relation to the Covenants, the latter cordially responded, and appointed a committee, with Dr. Goold as convener. This committee rendered valuable aid in the work of the joint-committee.

In 1873, the Reformed Presbyterian Synod was delicately situated. Each of the larger churches, it was understood, was willing to unite with it. After deliberation, it was agreed to approach the Free Church. In 1874 overtures were laid on the table of the General Assembly of that church proposing that steps should be taken towards Union. Both the Unionists and the Anti-Unionists cordially concurred. Committees were eventually appointed, and details speedily arranged. The only point regarding business details that we need notice is that the Reformed Presbyterian Synod continues to exist, to deal with civil rights and properties. Both churches entered into Union, conserving their distinctive principles and historical position. The smaller church was willing to accept the name of the larger and also

The Reformed Presbyterians 159

its Formula, on the understanding that the Act of the Assembly of the Church of Scotland, 1647, regarding the second article of the thirty-first chapter of the Westminster Confession was still in force, and that the Formula be read in the light of the Act of the Free Assembly, 1846. The Supreme Courts of both churches met at the same time in May 1876. The Uniting Act was agreed to with acclamation in the larger church. In the smaller, one minister dissented, the Rev. Thomas Easton, Stranraer. He stood alone for eleven years, and when he died, in 1887, his congregation joined the smaller Reformed Presbyterian Church. The congregation of Carnoustie returned to the Original Seceders, to whom it had formerly belonged, and that of Liverpool joined the English Presbyterians.

On 25th May the Union was consummated. The principal clerks, Sir Henry Wellwood Moncreiff, Bart., and Dr. William Wilson, both of whom were ex-Moderators, by the instruction of their Assembly, proceeded to the Martyrs'

Church, George IV. Bridge, where the Synod was assembled, and announced that the Free Assembly was ready to receive them. Thirty-five ministers and thirty-four elders, sixty-nine in all, the representatives of the church of the Hillmen and Societies marched two and two to the Assembly Hall. Thus they approached that building, from the towers of which waved the Union Jack and the blue banner of the Covenant. The crowd outside received them with a cheer. When they entered the hall in single file, the vast audience received them standing, in perfect silence. The reading of the Uniting Act, the moving of its adoption, the signing of it by the Moderators and clerks, and the election of Dr. Thomas MacLauchlan, the Moderator of the Free Assembly, as Moderator of the United Church, followed. The afternoon and evening were spent in the delivery of suitable addresses. The Reformed Presbyterian speakers were the Moderator, Dr. Goold, the Rev. John M'Dermid, Glasgow, the Rev. John Kay, Coatbridge,

The Reformed Presbyterians 161

their clerk, and Mr. Thomas Binnie, their treasurer. The Free Churchmen were Sheriff Campbell, their legal adviser, the Rev. Dr. Nelson, Greenock, of Reformed Presbyterian parentage, the Rev. Edward Thomson, Edinburgh, who had been an Original Seceder, Principal Rainy, and Drs. Begg and Duff. An interesting feature of the proceedings was the presence of representatives of the United Presbyterian and English Presbyterian Churches. Congratulatory addresses were delivered by Professor Calderwood, Edinburgh, the Rev. John Rankine, Cupar-Fife, Moderator of the United Presbyterian Synod, Dr. Cairns, and Dr. Oswald Dykes of London. The thrilling address of the last named produced a deep impression.

Among the ministers who entered into the Union, in addition to those named, should be mentioned the Rev. J. H. Thomson of Eaglesham, afterwards of Hightae, editor of *The Reformed Presbyterian Magazine*, and author of *The Martyr Graves of Scotland*. One congregation, that of Douglas, lost its buildings on account of the Union. Of the ministers who entered the Assembly Hall on the 28th of May 1876, most have passed to their reward. There are only ten of them now on the roll of the United Free Church. Dr. Goold was elected Moderator of the Free Church Assembly, 1877.

Thus the oldest of the non-Established Presbyterian Churches of Scotland, the one that claimed the closest kinship with the martyrs of the XVII century, from Argyll and Guthrie to Renwick, merged herself in the youngest and largest. If we remember aright, there appeared at the time of the Union in one of the newspapers of the day a poem in which an elderly man, of sad and sombre countenance, wearing a shepherd's plaid, is described as gazing into the grave of the Covenant. This is poetic licence. True, the Covenants are not named in the Act of Union. They are no longer considered binding on the descendants of those who framed and signed them. But the scriptural principles on which they are based, and which are contained in them, still live. The Free Church, in entering into the Union, left them again an open question. But she then took another step in advance. In 1852 she seemed to homologate the position of the Erskines, which was hardly consistent with the Revolution Settlement. In 1876, by making reference in the Act of Union to the Act of 1647, an Act ignored by the Revolution Settlement, does she not take her stand on the Second Reformation, on the scriptural principles held by Henderson, Rutherford, and Gillespie, in the palmy days of the Covenant, and during the Theocracy of the middle of the XVII century? Does not this action invalidate the historical positions of the Claim of Right? Have not the Hillmen and Society men, as in 1843, again triumphed? At anyrate, though we have not here a declaration on Creed first and Church second, or Church first and Creed second, we have Spiritual Independence first, State Connection second, and historical documents third.

CHAPTER XIII.

DECLARATORY ACTS—THE FREE PRESBYTERIANS, 1876-1900.

THERE remains only one date—the last on the cover of the *Missionary Record*—to consider. Before doing so, let us take a rapid review of the history of the United Presbyterian and Free Churches during the last quarter of the XIX century. During that period the work of both Churches advanced. The membership and the number of their congregations increased. So did their contributions. Their Missions abroad prospered. After the suspension of the Union negotiations, the United Presbyterians acquired their new Synod Buildings in Castle Terrace, Edinburgh. They also reconstructed their Divinity Hall, substituting Winter for Summer Sessions, and relieving their

Declaratory Acts

Professors from holding pastoral charges. The venerable Dr. Harper was appointed Principal. He and Dr. Cairns lectured on Theology, Dr. David Duff on Church History, Dr. Robert Johnstone on New Testament Exegesis, Professor James Paterson on Hebrew, and Dr. John Ker on Pastoral Theology. The Union of 1847 worked admirably. Perhaps fewer small congregations were amalgamated than was expected. But ministers, members, and congregations alike, learned to forget whether they had been Seceders or Relief, and to consider themselves simply United Presbyterians. The Free Church was agitated by a discussion of critical questions connected chiefly with the Old Testament, occasioned by objections taken in certain quarters to the teaching of some of the Professors. We refer to this as it bears on events to which we must allude later on. The two Churches held their jubilees, amid much enthusiasm—the Free Church in 1893, under the Moderatorship of the poet and preacher, Dr. Walter C. Smith of Edinburgh; the United Presbyterian in 1897, under that of Dr. Hutchison of Bonnington. On both occasions, deputations were received from sister Churches at home and in the Colonies. Both Churches espoused the cause of Disestablishment, not from any feeling of antagonism to the Church of Scotland as a branch of the Christian Church, but on other and wider grounds. In the Free Church there has always been on this question a minority, not large, but consistent.

Both Churches passed what are known as the Declaratory Acts, corresponding somewhat to the Testimonies of bygone days. Difficulties had arisen in the minds of several regarding the sense in which certain articles of the Westminster Confession were to be understood, and scruples were entertained about the adjustment of these to the living faith of the close of the XIX century. These points were brought under the notice of the Supreme Courts in the usual way, by overtures. Committees were appointed. The Acts were eventually framed and

Declaratory Acts 167

approved of. The United Presbyterians took action first. The subject was introduced into the Synod in 1877, the final stage being reached in 1879, two years later. The Free Church Committee was appointed in 1889, and the Act passed in 1892. The substance of both Acts was similar. The points dealt with belong to the same departments of Theology as those discussed in the Marrow Controversy and the Atonement Controversy in the Secession—the love and sovereignty of God in man's redemption; the responsibility of the hearers of the Gospel; predestination; the possibility of the salvation of infants, heathens, and all who have never heard the Gospel; the corruption of human nature. There is also a paragraph in each about the old question of the Civil Magistrate. Liberty is also recognised regarding questions that do not enter into the substance of the faith. The Free Church specifies none; the United Presbyterian selects as an example the six days of Creation.

These Acts were not, by either Church,

made binding on the entrants to office. In the smaller Church the second question put, on admission to office, ran thus: "Do you acknowledge the Westminster Confession of Faith and the Larger and Shorter Catechisms as an exhibition of the sense in which you understand the Holy Scriptures, this acknowledgment being made in view of the explanations contained in the Declaratory Act of Synod thereanent?" In the larger Church an Act was passed by the Assembly in 1894, declaring that "the Statements of doctrine contained in the said Act are not imposed upon any of the Church's office-bearers as part of the Standard of the Church, but that those who are licensed or ordained to office in answering the questions and subscribing the formula are entitled to do so in view of the said Declaratory Act." The Act of 1892 was passed in the Free Assembly by a majority of 151, the figures being 346 to 195. The minority, consisting largely of North-country ministers and elders, were satisfied with dissenting and protesting. Two ministers, however, seceded—the Rev. Donald Macfarlane, Raasay, in the Presbytery of Skye, and the late Rev. Donald MacDonald of Shieldaig, in the Presbytery of Lochcarron. In the following year, 1893, they, along with an elder, constituted a Presbytery, and assumed to themselves the name of the Free Presbyterian Church of Scotland. At the commencement of this year (1906) they have three Presbyteries with twenty charges, fourteen ministers, and a foreign missionary whose sphere of labour is in Rhodesia. Most of their congregations are situated in the North and West of Scotland.

CHAPTER XIV.

THE UNION OF THE FREE AND THE UNITED PRESBYTERIAN CHURCHES, 1900.

WE have now arrived at the last date on the cover of the *Record*—1900—that of the Union of the Free and United Presbyterian Churches. These two had gradually been drawing closer to each other. In 1893, the year of the jubilee of the Free Church, corresponding members of each Church sat in the Supreme Court of the other with all rights except that of voting. In the following year overtures on the subject of union were laid on the table of the Assembly. Both courts proceeded cautiously. A proposal for a larger union, including the Establishment, was set aside. In 1897 it was agreed that an Advisory Committee be appointed to deal

The Union of the Churches

with questions of practical business in which both churches were interested. In the same year the committees on Union were instructed to consider the basis of Union. Their recommendations were practically approved of by the Superior Courts, May 1900,—in the Synod unanimously, in the Assembly by 593 to 29, the minority consisting of seventeen ministers and twelve elders. The Uniting Act, with relative documents, was sent down to Presbyteries for approval. It was also agreed that the United Church should be called the United Free Church of Scotland.

On the 30th day of October 1900. the United Presbyterian Church held an *in hunc effectum* meeting of Synod (her last meeting of Synod), and a duly elected Assembly of the Free Church met. That day the Uniting Act was passed, in the one again unanimously (the members standing and holding up their right hands), in the other by a majority of 643 to 27. After the vote in the Assembly, there was read and signed by four ministers and three elders a protest which we shall notice presently. At the close of these meetings, both courts adjourned, to meet the next day in the Waverley Market at half-past eleven.

The last day of October of the concluding year of the XIX century was the day selected for the largest ecclesiastical Union that has as yet taken place in the history of Scotland. The morning and early forenoon were wet, the after part dull. The place of meeting was not, like some of those chosen on former occasions, associated with previous events in the religious history of the country, but, like Tanfield Hall in 1843, unconnected with the past. This seems to indicate on the face of it that the Union marks a new departure, fraught with good to the religious, ecclesiastical, moral and social interests of the nation. The past, however, was not forgotten. The original Covenant of 1638, swords and banners connected with the period of the persecutions, and other relics of bygone days were displayed in the hall. Early in the

The Union of the Churches 173

day, the members of the United Presbyterian Synod met in their hall in Castle Terrace and marched in couples by the Lothian Road and Princes Street to the Mound, where they were joined by the other procession, which had gathered in the quadrangle of the New College. There they joined and walked four abreast. The procession was headed by the two Moderators, Dr. Alexander Mair of Morningside, Edinburgh, and Dr. Walter Ross Taylor of Kelvinside, Glasgow, and by Dr. James Stewart of Lovedale, the well-known Missionary Moderator of the Free Church in 1899, and Dr. Alexander Oliver, Regent Place, Glasgow, Moderator of the United Presbyterian Synod in 1894. The event was witnessed by thousands of spectators.

By half-past eleven the Waverley Market was fully occupied by the members and general public. At that hour Dr. Taylor took the chair, Dr. Mair being at his right hand and the other officials in their places. The audience rose to receive them. The

Moderator commenced the proceedings by giving out the well-known words of Psalm cxxxiii., which were sung by the audience, and he then constituted the Assembly by prayer. Dr. Mair read Ephesians iv. and constituted the Synod also by prayer. The minutes of the two courts were read by the clerks. The adoption of the Uniting Act was moved by Dr. James Murray Mitchell, who had been sent to Bombay by the Church of Scotland, had occupied the unique position of serving the Free Church in the home, foreign and continental fields, and was the third oldest minister of the Free Church. The motion was seconded by Dr. Andrew Henderson, Paisley, the first minister ordained after the Union of 1847, and thus the oldest son of the United Presbyterian Church, and Moderator of Synod in 1891. Thereafter the deliverance was unanimously adopted, the members standing and holding up their right hands. Dr. Taylor, in solemn tones, declared the Churches one in the following words: "In the presence of our Divine King and Head,

The Union of the Churches

the King and Head of the Church, and with the concurrence of my brother Moderator, I declare the Act of Union finally adopted, and that the Free Church of Scotland and the United Presbyterian Church are now one Church in Christ Jesus under the designation of the United Free Church of Scotland." The Assembly having sung the closing verses of the seventy-second Psalm. Dr. Taylor, turning to Dr. Mair, addressed him thus: "It is now my high privilege, in the name of the Free Church of Scotland, to offer you, honoured brother, as Moderator of the United Presbyterian Synod, the right hand of fellowship in token of the happy union now formed betwixt the two Churches." Dr. Mair responded in similar terms. Dr. Taylor then said: "May the Three, One God, the Father, Son and Holy Spirit richly bless the United Free Church of Scotland," and Dr. Mair added: "and make her a blessing to Scotland and to the world, and a glory to her Lord and King." To these words each of the Moderators added his Amen. The Uniting Act was then signed by the officials amid prolonged applause. Dr. Taylor thereupon constituted the United Assembly by prayer, and the Rolls of the Synod and the Assembly were recognised as the Roll of the Assembly.

The first business was the election of a Moderator. Only one name had been thought of in this connection, that of Principal Robert Rainy of the New College, Edinburgh. Born on 1st January 1826, he is the son of a Professor of Forensic Medicine in the University of Glasgow, and was minister successively of Huntly and the Free High Church, Edinburgh. He succeeded Principal Cunningham, in 1862, as Professor of Church History in the New College, and Principal Candlish, in 1874, as head of that college. He had been since the death of Dr. Robert Buchanan, two years after the suspension of the Union negotiations, the acknowledged leader of the Free Church. As an ecclesiastical statesman he combines many of the qualities

The Union of the Churches

of Henderson and Carstairs. He is well-known among the Churches of the Reformation for his theological and general learning, his spirituality and high character as a Christian gentleman and minister. His name is irrevocably identified with the Union of 1900. Dr. Mair, in nominating him for the chair, spoke of him as having "taken a pre-eminent position in carrying out the Union negotiations." Dr. Mair also mentioned that of the fifty-three members of the Free Church Union Committee of 1863 Dr. Rainy was sole survivor.

It is unnecessary to dwell in detail on the proceedings of the Assembly. They lasted two days, and a good deal of business was done. Thirty-nine congratulatory addresses were received, including many from churches in England, Scotland and the Colonies. Several representatives of these churches and other guests addressed the Assembly. Among these may be mentioned the late Dr. Joseph Parker of London, Principal Fairbairn of Mansfield College, Oxford, Drs. Alexander M'Laren of Manchester, John Watson of Liverpool, and Cameron Lees of Edinburgh, and the Earl of Aberdeen, grandson of the Earl of 1843, and Lord Kinnaird.

The Union is based on the Westminster standards. There were no Articles of Agreement formulated. The churches practically took each other as they stood. To understand fully the Uniting Act we must read it in the light of four Declarations accepted by each of the churches before the Union and in that of the Questions to be put to office-bearers on admission. We must now direct attention to two or three points suggested by them. In the third Declaration it is distinctly stated that the members of both Churches "shall have full right, as they see cause, to assert and maintain the views of truth and duty which they had liberty to maintain in the said Churches." Here no new restriction is imposed on either side. The Larger and Shorter Catechisms had been regarded by the United Presbyterians as Standards along with the Westminster

The Union of the Churches 179

Confession, and their office-bearers were required to give their assent to them. They are now dropped out of the Questions by the United Church and relegated to the second Declaration, wherein they are described "as manuals of religious instruction long approved and held in honour by the people of both churches." Thus the number of authorised documents was further diminished.

The question regarding the Confession is also altered. The United Presbyterians had spoken of the Confession as an exhibition of the sense in which the Holy Scriptures are to be understood, the Free Church of the whole doctrine contained in the Confession "approvan by former General Assemblies." The United Church speaks of "the doctrine of the Church set forth in the Confession . . ." This is practically saying the Church first the Confession second. She does not accept the doctrine of the Confession. the Confession contains the doctrine of the Church. Whatever may have been the private opinions of the fathers of the

Secession and Disruption this is a distinct advance on 1733 and 1843.

The two Declaratory Acts are associated with the Confession. They are not mentioned, it is true, in the questions. But the Preamble prefixed to these distinctly states, that the "questions are put in view of Act 1647 approving of the Confession of faith, Act XII., 1846, of the Free Church of Scotland, Declaratory Act, 1879, of the United Presbyterian Church, and Act XII.. 1892, with relative Act of 1894 of the Free Church, and that ministers are entitled to avail themselves of any of these Acts." The Act of 1647 is inserted, probably on account of the union of the Reformed Presbyterians with the Free Church. No minister is asked to assent to these Declaratory Acts, but he is entitled to avail himself of them in his own interpretation of the Confession.

The only other reference to historical documents is in Question IV. addressed to ministers, and the corresponding one put to elders and probationers. We quote

The Union of the Churches

it in full: "Do you believe that the Lord Jesus Christ, as King and Head of the Church, has therein appointed a government in the hands of church officers, distinct from, and not subordinate in its own province to civil government, and that the Civil Magistrate does not possess jurisdiction or authoritative control over the regulation of the affairs of Christ's Church; and do you approve of the general principles with respect to the spirituality and freedom of the Church of Christ, and her subjection to Him as her only Head, and to His Word as her only Standard, embodied in the Claim of Right of 1842, the Protest of 1843, and the basis of Union of 1847, as principles which are sanctioned by the Word of God and the subordinate Standards of this Church?" Here, as in the Churches singly, office-bearers are bound only to the general principles of the spirituality and freedom of the Church and her subjection to Christ and His Word.

In the latest and greatest Union, as in

the Separations and former Unions, we have Spiritual Independence first and State connection second. The United Free Church is in a Christian sense proud of her ancestry. She cherishes the sacred memories that gather round it. But, unlike her component parts, she does not anchor herself to documents such as Covenants, Testimonies, Claims of Right, or even unduly to Confessions, or to facts, such as Revolution Settlements, Secessions, Disruptions. She accepts these in so far as they affect her work and historic continuity. She adheres, however, to the Scriptural principles embodied in the documents and exemplified in the facts. Forgetting the things that are behind, yet carrying her past with her, she reaches forward to those that are before. The principles are the living stream, the documents are the banks of the stream, but the stream occasionally overflows the banks. The principles are the spirit that animates the Church, the documents are the garments that clothe her. If the principles for a season lose

The Union of the Churches

their power, the garments become unduly binding, they almost become grave clothes. When the principles recover their power the garments may need to be changed, for they must be the embodiment of the life of the Church. The Church is subject to Christ her only Head and His Word her only standard. Such is the United Free Church of Scotland.

The two Churches entered into the Union with their divinity halls, professors, missionaries to the Jews and in India, China, Africa, New Hebrides, and elsewhere, and with all their arrangements and agencies at home and abroad in working order. The membership of the smaller Church was 199,089, of the larger 296,085. The contributions of the one amounted to £472,638, and of the other £706,546. The congregations in the one numbered 597, in the other 1062, with home mission stations; the ministers 637 and 1144.

Of the Free Church ministers who had been ordained in the Establishment, those who survived were the Rev. James

Yule, Peterhead, ordained 1835; the Rev. James Murray Mitchell, D.D., Nice, 1838; the Rev. Thomas Smith, D.D., Edinburgh, 1839, Moderator in 1891; the Rev. David Paton, Fettercairn, 1841; the Rev. Alexander Rankine, Strathaven, 1842. There was another Disruption minister living in America, the Rev. William Ferrie, Anstruther, 1839. There were other two ministers in the Free Church ordained before 1843 who were not in the Establishment, the Rev. Adam Ross, Rattray, 1838, original Burgher, who had been Moderator of that Synod when it joined the Original Anti-Burghers in 1842, and the Rev. Robert Gault, Glasgow, 1840. who had been ordained in Ireland. Of these, only Mr. Ross and Dr. Smith are now spared (1906).

In the United Presbyterian Synod there were thirteen who had been ordained before the Union of the Secession and Relief — the Rev. Robert Frew, D.D., St. Ninians, Relief, ordained 1835, Moderator in 1868; Andrew Thomson, D.D., Broughton Place, Edinburgh,

The Union of the Churches

Secession, 1837. Moderator in 1874; John F. Cumming, Emgwali, Kaffraria, Relief, 1839; the Rev. David Anderson, Ceres, Relief, 1840; George Alison, Kilbarchan, Relief, 1842; James Fleming, Whithorn, Secession, 1842, Moderator in 1890; Henry A. Paterson, Stonehouse, Secession, 1842; William Lauder, Port Glasgow, Secession, 1842; Andrew W. Smith, Pitlessie, Secession, 1844; John B. Ritchie, Charlotte Street, Aberdeen, Secession, 1845; James Fitzpatrick, Lisburn, Ireland, Associate Presbytery of Ireland, 1846; John Mitchell, Kirkintilloch, Relief, 1846; Peter Mearns, Coldstream, Secession, 1846. Of these only five remain, Dr. Frew, Messrs. Cumming, Anderson, Ritchie, and Fitzpatrick. Dr. Frew is the first father of the United Free Church, and the survivor of the United Presbyterian Union Committee of 1863. After a separate existence of fully fifty-three years, the "United Presbyterian," and after fully fifty-seven the "Free," merged themselves in the "United Free." These names will be retained for a season within the United Church in connection with some of the funds or associations, but in fifty years, or little more, they will be like Burgher and Anti-Burgher, Secession and Relief, Original Secession and Reformed Presbyterian—names and memories of the past.

CHAPTER XV.

THE FREE CHURCH OF 1900.

VARIOUS results must follow the Union of 1900. Some of these will be unexpected. One that has occurred can hardly be said to have been looked for. It has been brought about by the action of the minority of the Free Church. That minority was always small. As the Union approached, it diminished in numbers. Several acquiesced and adhered to the Union. Speaking of the remainder generally, they had opposed the Declaratory Act, and therefore, perhaps, should have gone out with the Free Presbyterians. They had not approved of the manner in which the Assembly had dealt with the alleged teaching of the professors in connection with the Higher Criticism. They followed the example of those who had taken part in former Separations. The

Erskines did not join the Reformed Presbyterians, nor Gillespie the Erskines, nor the leaders of 1843 the Seceders or Relief. Likewise this new minority did not unite with the remnant Reformed Presbyterians, or Original Seceders, or even with the Free Presbyterians. They in their protest held that the majority had withdrawn from the Free Church, and they claimed for themselves the right to carry on the business of the Assembly and the work of the Church.

On the day of the Union. after failing to gain admission to the hall on the Mound, they met in the Queen Street Hall, and selected as their Moderator the Rev. Colin A. Bannatyne, Coulter, the only lowland country minister adhering to them. Their Assembly sat for three days. Including some who had retired from active duty, the number of adhering ministers was twenty-seven. Two of them were in Edinburgh, three in Glasgow, and the remainder of those on active duty were, with the exception of Mr. Bannatyne, resident in the High-

The Free Church of 1900

lands and Northern Counties. About 16,000 people were claimed to have joined them, and these chiefly belonged to the North and West of Scotland. It may be asked here in passing, did these gentlemen deliberately break their ordination vows? They were bound to submit to the Church Courts, and to assent to the principles regarding Spiritual Independence contained in the Claim of Right, principles the majority had not denied. Having declared that the other party had left the Free Church, they certainly could not complain when they themselves were cut off by that party. As Dr. Charles M'Crie has said, "had they fallen into the hands of Adam Gib, their punishment would have been nothing short of suspension, and even of deposition."

Within six weeks of the Union the action known as Bannatyne v. Overtoun was raised: in this the smaller body claimed all the property of the Free Church. As is well known, the action was decided against them in the Scottish

Courts, but in their favour by the House of Lords, 1st August 1904. The final disposal of the property is now in the hands of a Parliamentary Commission. Into this aspect of the question we are not called upon to enter, except perhaps to note that the litigation arose in connection with the perennial question of the relation of the Civil Magistrate to the Church.

Let us look at the bearing of this judgment on the points that have been before us. The decision of the Supreme Court, while depriving the larger portion of the United Free Church of its property, does not interfere with the independence of that Church. Its relation to its Confession and other documents remains unaffected, unless some dispute about property occur in the future. The Civil Court seems to have loosened the hold which the shadow of the Revolution Settlement and other Acts of Parliament may be said to have had on that Church. The United Free General Assembly of 1905, the first held after the decision of the Supreme Court of the previous year, may be looked upon as the freest Assembly Scotland has seen since the fifth decade of the XVII century.

The case of the smaller church is different from, almost the reverse of, that of the other. The Court of Appeal, while adjudging to them their property, seems at their own instigation to have limited their Spiritual Independence. To understand this we must remember the grounds of the opposition to the Union. These appear to be fourfold—the Establishment principle, the Declaratory Act, the teaching of the professors, and the use of uninspired hymns and instrumental music. On the last two we are not called upon to enter, as they are not directly referred to in the proceedings on the day preceding the Union, nor in the pleadings before the Courts of Law. Suffice it to say, that the Acts of the General Assembly, regarding hymns and musical instruments, as well as those regarding the Declaratory Act, were repealed in

1905 by the Assembly of this Free Church of 1900 and 1904.

Let us look at the other two. In the motion made by the Rev. Mr. Bannatyne, on 30th October 1900, in opposition to the passing of the Uniting Act, the distinctive principles of the Free Church are stated to be "the whole superior and secondary Standards of the Church in their entirety," and the special testimony in regard to Establishments as contained in the Claim of Right.

The Standards here referred to are the Word of God and the Westminster Confession, but the questions naturally arise, which of them is to interpret the other? Is the Confession to be interpreted by the Word, or the Word to be interpreted, in any point that may be in dispute, by the Confession? Can the Church, in her legislative capacity, interpret her own Confession, by Declaratory Acts or otherwise? If she cannot do the latter there is a danger that the saying of Lord MacNaughton that "the supreme and ultimate standard of doctrine is not the Bible but the Confession of Faith," may prove true. This looks like infallibility. It is at least the finality of the Westminster Confession. Which is to be preferred?

Special stress throughout all these discussions was laid on the other point, the Establishment principle, or, as it may be called, the application of the doctrine of the Supremacy of the Redeemer over all things, to the relation between Church and State. The question whether this is in the Westminster Confession is a debatable one. In the well-known Campbeltown case, where the ownership of a Relief Church was in dispute, three judges, Lord-Justice Clerk Boyle, afterwards Lord President, and Lords Meadowbank and Medwyn, inclined to the opinion that it was not. The soundness of this was questioned by Lord Robertson in the Court of Appeal in 1904, upwards of sixty years later. The judges above mentioned, it may be noted, had given their opinions in the Auchterarder Case against the General Assembly of the Church of Scotland.

But it is said that Establishment is contained in the Claim of Right, and that opinion has now been endorsed by the Supreme Court of Appeal. The Claim, as we have already seen, contains the interpretation of the Revolution Settlement by the founders of the Free Church, an interpretation rejected by the Courts of Law, the House of Commons, and the ministers of the Crown. The Free Church of 1904 is bound, by the House of Lords, through its own action, to what may be called, with all respect, a semi-illegal document, and, to say the least of it, a semi-Erastian settlement. The Claim may have been suitable for the middle of last century, it is hardly so for the beginning of this. Is the conception of the relation between Church and State embodied in it ideal, perfect, final for Scotland in all time coming? We never heard that descending obligations on posterity were claimed for it as for the National Covenant. If they are, why not accept those of the greater document rather than the lesser? We are inclined to agree with the position taken by the venerable Dr. Thomas Smith in his article in *Young Scotland* (January 1905), that "Mr. Bannatyne and his associates go a step, a long stride, further than Dr. Cook," of the Disruption days, "and his followers. They deny that autonomy is good. They owe their position to the assumption that it is positively evil." Dr. Cook seemed to prefer State connection to Spiritual Independence. Does the Free Church do the same?

In this last controversy we meet with the same two points as in the former ones—the Civil Magistrate, and the mode of presenting the Gospel to its hearers. The mistake of the Free Church of 1900 and 1904 is that of the older Reformed Presbyterian, and Seceders, and also of the Free Presbyterians, in anchoring themselves to documents and events, rather than to scriptural principles; to the Westminster Confession of the English Puritans and the Revolution Settlement, the Claim of Rights and the Disruption, rather than to the scriptural principles of preaching the Love and Sovereignty of God combined, and the Mediatorial Headship over all of the Incarnate Son of God.

CHAPTER XVI.

CONCLUSION.

OUR review of the Story of Two Hundred and Twenty-five Years is now completed. We have endeavoured to explain the origin and trace in outline the history of the various component parts of the United Free Church of Scotland,—the Reformed Presbyterian, the Secession, the Relief and the Free Church, in their separations and unions. We have seen that they owe their separate origins to similar causes, and that their histories have run in similar courses. They have had to deal with the two questions of the Civil Magistrate and the mode of presenting the Gospel. As each separated from the National Establishment, it did not join at first any of the other non-Established Churches then existing. It formed a new organisation; each anchored itself, perhaps unduly, to documents and events. As years glided past, each grew broader and more liberal —the later ones more rapidly than the earlier. They could not enter into Unions without some separation, however small, and in most cases left behind them those who maintained in their entirety their former contendings. Now the various streams flow together in one deep bed, in one wide channel. They are merged, and will soon be lost and forgotten in one mighty river. When we look at the United Church we remember the words of the Apostle to the Corinthians: "All things are yours, whether Paul, Apollos or Cephas." May we not paraphrase them thus: All are yours, all the hallowed memories that hover round the past of the various component parts, all the work of that past done for Scotland and for Christ; Cameron, Renwick, M'Millan and the Societies; the Erskines, their coadjutors, and the Secession; Gillespie, his successors and the Relief; the M'Cries, the Symingtons, the Goolds; Chalmers, his contemporaries, older and younger, who influenced the life of the second half of last century and the Disruption; not to speak of the numerous theologians, preachers, missionaries, authors, who have gone to their rest and reward, and whose work the Church will not willingly forget. All are yours. The courage of Cameron, the steadfastness of Ebenezer Erskine, the meekness of Gillespie, the catholicity of Chalmers, are the Heritage of the United Free Church. The Church also possesses a culture wider and greater than that of the Moderates of the XVIII century. May these all be found blended in it in symmetrical proportion. Looking back, we see a strange and striking combination, we might almost say extremes meeting. The outside position of the Hillmen has triumphed all along the line, and so has the spirit manifested by the ejected minister of Carnock, who devoted himself entirely to the preaching of a free and full Gospel. May the spirit of Thomas Gillespie pervade the Church of 1900.

It is interesting to note that the oldest minister at the Union, Dr. Robert Frew,

St. Ninians, belonged to the Relief. He is still spared to us—seventy years a minister, the father of the Church, the oldest minister in Scotland, the only one ordained before the accession of Queen Victoria. In the words of the Moderators on the Union day, "May the Three, One God, the Father, Son, and Holy Spirit, richly bless the United Free Church of Scotland, and make her a blessing to Scotland and to the world, and a glory to her Lord and King. Amen and Amen."

We will not attempt to predict the future. The unexpected so often happens. But it may be permitted, ere we conclude, to advert briefly to two points in the line of argument we have been pursuing.

The one is that the Churches and the State must adjust their Confessions to the living faith and in the living words of the XX century. A step has already been taken in the right direction in the passing by Parliament of the fifth clause of the "Churches (Scotland) Act, 1905," in which it is declared that the formula of subscription to the Confession in the

Church of Scotland shall be prescribed by the General Assembly with the consent of Presbyteries. This, of course, is in harmony with the Revolution Settlement. That Settlement cannot be interfered with lightly or hastily in any of its fundamental positions. The Confession occupies a peculiar position. It is the Confession of the nation, has its place on the Statute Book, and, of course, can be interpreted, like all other Statutes, by the Courts of the land. It is imposed by Parliament on the National Church, and is interpreted by its Courts in all cases that come before them in which doctrine is involved. It has been adopted by the non-Established Presbyterian Churches, of their own free will, as their Confession, and they interpret it for themselves; thus, without intending it, interpreting the law of the land. Their right to do this has never been questioned, except, perhaps, where property is involved. Their right to do this seems to have been tacitly acknowledged. It may always be said to be recognised in the "Churches Act, 1905."

This state of things seems anomalous. A Confession is an ecclesiastical document embodying an expression of the religious faith of the Church. Should a State have such a document, or at least one so minute as the Westminster? The possession of it may have been suitable to the XVI and XVII centuries, or even to the XVIII or early part of the XIX, when Tests were in force. But it is hardly suitable to the XX. Might it not be removed from the Statute Book and treated simply as the Confession of the Churches? This would not necessarily affect the Establishment of the Church. The State could recognise it as the Confession of the Established Church, and even make the retention of it a condition of State connection. An arrangement of this kind might simplify the situation.

Our second point is briefly this: the Church should lift up a testimony for the Mediatorial Sovereignty of the Incarnate Son of God. He is the living Head, the sole King and Head of His Church. But He is also Head of all things to His Church. He is the Messiah King. By Him " Kings reign and princes decree justice." By Him " Princes rule, and nobles, even all the judges of the earth." Is He not their Head, His Word their Standard? This truth all civil rulers ought to acknowledge. To keep them in remembrance of it is the duty of the Christian Church. When that duty is discharged by the one, and that truth realised by the other, will not the scriptural principles underlying the course of action pursued by the Covenanters, the principles of the Hillmen, have triumphed? For the Father hath committed all things into the hands of the Son, the Incarnate One, the Lion of the Tribe of Judah, the Prince of the House of David, the Priest upon His Throne, the Lamb in the midst of the Throne on whose Head are many Crowns, the Risen, Ascended, and Glorified Christ, to whom be ascribed, with the Father and the Holy Spirit, glory and majesty, dominion and power, for ever and ever. Amen.

APPENDIX I.

THE CHILDREN'S BOND.

DR. HAY FLEMING in his *Story of the Scottish Covenants*, writes thus:—"One of the most curious and suggestive documents of this period is known as 'The Children's Bond.' In 1683, "when there was no faithful minister in Scotland," a number of children in the village of Pentland, who had formed themselves into a society for devotional purposes, solemnly entered into a covenant, of which the following is a copy:—

"This is a covenant made between the Lord and us, with our whole hearts, and to give up ourselves freely to Him, without reserve, soul and body, hearts and affections, to be His children, and Him to be our God and Father, if it please the holy Lord to send His Gospel to the land again; that we stand to this covenant which we have written between the Lord and us, as we shall answer at the great day, that we shall never break this covenant which we have made between the Lord and us; that we shall stand to this

APPENDIX II.

COMPARATIVE TABLE indicating the relative proportion of the ministers separating from and adhering to the Scottish Establishment in 1662 and in 1843.

[The first column (marked N.M.), under 1662 and 1843 respectively, indicates the number of ministers in the Presbytery at the time; the second column (marked V.), vacant charges; the third column (marked S.), ministers separating; the fourth column (marked A.), ministers adhering.]

I.—SYNOD OF LOTHIAN AND TWEEDALE.

Presbyteries.	1662.				1843.			
	N.M.	V.	S.	A.	N.M.	V.	S.	A.
Edinburgh	23	5	14	9	55	1	34	21
Linlithgow	19	2	8	11	22	1	5	17
Biggar	14	0	12	2	11	0	2	9
Peebles	14	0	3	11	12	0	3	9
Dalkeith	16	0	5	11	19	3	5	14
Haddington	14	2	3	11	20	0	11	9
Dunbar	9	1	1	8	11	0	4	7
Total in Synod	109	10	46	63	150	5	64	86

Appendix II

II.—Synod of Merse and Teviotdale.

Presbyteries.	1662.				1843.			
	N.M.	V.	S.	A.	N.M.	V.	S.	A.
Duns	9	2	2	7	12	0	6	6
Chirnside	13	1	5	8	13	0	3	10
Kelso	10	0	2	8	11	0	2	9
Jedburgh	16	1	11	5	15	0	3	12
Lauder	9	0	5	4	9	0	1	8
Selkirk	10	0	7	3	13	0	3	10
Total in Synod	67	4	32	35	73	0	18	55

III.—Synod of Dumfries.

Dumfries	17	1	16	1	24	0	6	18
Annan	6	2	3	3	11	0	3	8
Langholm	6	0	3	3	7	0	1	6
Lochmaben	13	0	6	7	13	0	1	12
Penpont	10	0	6	4	9	1	2	7
Total in Synod	52	3	34	18	64	1	13	51

IV.—Synod of Galloway.

Kirkcudbright	16	0	15	1	17	0	3	14
Wigtown	10	0	8	2	11	0	1	10
Stranraer	10	1	9	1	13	0	5	8
Total in Synod	36	1	32	4	41	0	9	32

V.—Synod of Glasgow and Ayr.

Glasgow	17	0	14	3	58	7	31	27
Ayr	30	1	27	3	37	0	11	26
Carry forward	47	1	41	6	95	7	42	53

Appendix II

	1662.				1843.			
Presbyteries	N.M	V.	S.	A.	N.M.	V.	S.	A.
Brought forward	47	1	41	6	95	7	42	53
Irvine	16	2	14	2	20	3	9	11
Paisley	11	1	11	0	22	1	10	12
Greenock	6	0	4	2	16	1	12	4
Hamilton	14	1	13	1	25	3	8	17
Lanark	11	1	7	4	16	0	3	13
Dumbarton	15	2	7	8	23	0	5	18
Total in Synod	120	8	97	23	217	15	89	128

VI.—Synod of Argyll.

Inveraray	6	0	5	1	6	2	0	6
Dunoon	9	0	4	5	11	0	7	4
Kintyre	5	3	5	0	10	1	3	7
Isla and Jura	0	3	0	0	6	1	2	4
Lorn	7	2	2	5	8	2	5	3
Mull	3	3	0	3	13	1	2	11
Total in Synod	30	11	16	14	54	7	19	35

VII.—Synod of Perth and Stirling

Dunkeld	14	1	5	9	13	1	7	6
Weem	6	0	1	5	11	1	4	7
Auchterarder	15	0	0	15	18	1	7	11
Perth	22	1	4	18	30	0	13	17
Stirling	11	1	2	9	16	3	10	6
Dunblane	12	0	1	11	16	1	7	9
Total in Synod	80	3	13	67	104	7	48	56

Appendix II

VIII.—Synod of Fife.

Presbyteries.	1662.				1843			
	N.M.	V.	S.	A	N.M.	V.	S.	A.
St. Andrews	19	2	15	4	22	1	5	17
Cupar	19	1	6	13	22	0	9	13
Kirkcaldy	18	0	5	13	21	1	9	12
Dunfermline	13	1	3	10	18	0	7	11
Total in Synod	69	4	29	40	83	2	30	53

IX.—Synod of Angus and Mearns

	N.M.	V.	S.	A	N.M.	V.	S.	A.
Dundee	18	0	3	15	29	1	15	14
Meigle	13	0	1	12	14	0	2	12
Forfar	11	0	1	10	12	1	3	9
Arbroath	11	0	0	11	17	0	9	8
Brechin	16	2	1	15	18	0	7	11
Fordoun	14	0	0	14	15	0	4	11
Total in Synod	83	2	6	77	105	2	40	65

X.—Synod of Aberdeen.

	N.M.	V.	S.	A	N.M.	V.	S.	A.
Aberdeen	17	2	2	15	36	0	19	17
Kincardine O'Neil	15	0	3	12	19	0	6	13
Alford	14	2	0	14	13	0	0	13
Garioch	16	0	0	16	16	1	4	12
Ellon	8	0	0	8	8	0	1	7
Deer	13	0	6	7	16	0	2	14
Turriff	11	1	1	10	12	0	5	7
Fordyce	7	0	0	7	12	0	7	5
Total in Synod	101	5	12	89	132	1	44	88

XI.—Synod of Moray.

| | 1662. | | | | 1843. | | | |
Presbyteries.	N.M.	V	S	A.	N.M.	V.	S.	A.
Elgin	12	0	2	10	12	0	4	8
Forres	6	0	1	5	6	0	4	2
Strathbogie	12	0	1	11	12	0	2	10
Aberlour	6	0	0	6	4	1	1	3
Abernethy	5	1	0	5	10	0	2	8
Nairn	5	1	1	4	6	0	3	3
Inverness	5	4	0	5	12	1	5	7
Total in Synod	51	6	5	46	62	2	21	41

XII.—Synod of Ross.

Chanonry	7	1	1	6	8	0	5	3
Dingwall	7	1	2	5	12	0	9	3
Tain	9	0	2	7	10	0	9	1
Total in Synod	23	2	5	18	30	0	23	7

XIII.—Synod of Sutherland and Caithness.

Dornoch	8	1	0	8	12	0	7	5
Tongue	1	1	0	1	7	0	5	2
Caithness	9	1	1	8	13	2	10	3
Total in Synod	18	3	1	17	32	2	22	10

XIV.—Synod of Glenelg.

Lochcarron	5	2	0	5	13	0	5	8
Abertarff	3	1	0	3	8	0	4	4
Skye	3	3	0	3	10	0	3	7
Uist	2	1	0	2	6	0	1	5
Lewis	1	1	0	1	6	0	4	2
Total in Synod	14	8	0	14	43	0	17	26

XV.—SYNOD OF ORKNEY.

Presbyteries.	1662.				1843.			
	N.M.	V.	S.	A.	N.M.	V.	S.	A
Kirkwall .	6	0	0	6	8	0	3	5
Cairston .	6	0	0	6	7	0	2	5
North Isles	6	0	1	5	8	0	2	6
Total in Synod	18	0	1	17	23	0	7	16

XVI.—SYNOD OF SHETLAND.

Lerwick .	5	0	0	5	9	0	4	5
Burravoe .	4	2	0	4	7	0	2	5
Total in Synod	9	2	0	9	16	0	6	10
Tot. Summation	880	72	329	551	1229	44	470	759

The portion of the above Tables relating to the earlier Exodus, that of 1662, was compiled from Dr. Hew Scott's *Fasti*, after the union of the Reformed Presbyterian Church with the Free Church, thirty years ago. We, of course, vouch only for its substantial accuracy. It differs in several respects from the list drawn out by Wodrow. According to Scott, about seventy ministers were banished, fined, or imprisoned. Only one, Donald Cargil, of the Barony, Glasgow, actually suffered martyrdom. About one hundred and fifty accepted indulgences. It would appear that upwards of two hundred survived the Revolution, almost equally divided between the two sections. It would be interesting to enter into further details, but space forbids.

The other portion of the Table is based on the *Annals of the Disruption; The Wheat and the Chaff*, by M'Cosh; the

Fasti, and the Edinburgh Almanacs of 1843 and 1844. The difficulty here has been to deal with Chapel of Ease ministers, the missionaries of the Society for the Propagation of Christian Knowledge, and those appointed by the Committee of the General Assembly for managing the Royal Bounty. None of these had seats in Church Courts. In most cases we have been guided by the fact of the name having been given by Dr. Scott. We have not reckoned among the separating ministers those that had retired, such as Dr. Charles Watson of Burntisland; Professors in the Arts Faculties, such as Drs. Robert Brown and John Fleming, both of Aberdeen; the Rev. Mr. Henry of Marnoch; and the ordained missionaries who preached in the parishes of the Strathbogie ministers that were deposed. Principal Cunningham of St. Andrews reckons the number of the clergy of the Established Church at 1203; 451 Seceders, of whom 289 were parish ministers; 162 Quoad Sacra. The remainder, 635 parish ministers, 117 Quoad Sacra, adhered to the Establishment.

The Tables bear out the statement that where the movement of 1662 was strong, that of 1843 was comparatively weak, and *vice-versa*. They suggest other points of comparison. We mention only two. Those Presbyteries that included within their bounds growing towns, had increased in the number of members on the roll during the one hundred and eighty years that had elapsed between 1662 and 1843. Several in rural districts remained stationary, or even slightly decreased, owing to the practice (carried on probably to a too large extent in the XVIII century) of uniting small contiguous parishes. The other point is this. The Tables illustrate the very inadequate provision made by the Church of the Reformation and the Covenant, for the people of the Northern Counties. But the want of space forbids our going into further detail. We venture to suggest that a valuable addition would be made to our Ecclesiastical Literature by the preparation of a revised edition of Dr. Scott's work, and its continuation up to date by competent local parties under the supervision of a Committee of the General Assembly of the Church of Scotland. Such a work would contain a good deal of curious, interesting, and instructive information, which could not fail to throw many a sidelight on the various periods of Scottish Church History.

APPENDIX III.

LIST OF MODERATORS AND PROFESSORS.

REFORMED PRESBYTERIAN SYNOD.

MODERATORS.

1811. John M'Millan (*Tertius*), Stirling, Professor.
1812. Archibald Mason, D.D., Wishaw.
1813. Thomas Henderson, Kilmalcolm
1814. John Reid, Lauriston.
1815. John Fairley, Glasgow.
1816. Thomas Rowatt, Penpont.
1817. Adam Brown, Kilmarnock.
1818 (May). William Goold, Edinburgh.
1818 (November.) Andrew Symington, D.D., Paisley, afterwards Professor.
1819. Archibald Rogerson, Darvel.
1820. John West, Colmonell.
1821. David Armstrong, Glasgow.
1822. John Fairley, Glasgow (second time)
1823. John Jeffray, Dumfries.
1824. John Osborne, Castle-Douglas
1825. Peter M'Indoe, D.D., Chirnside.
1826. William Symington, D.D., Stranraer.
1827. John Milwain, Douglas.
1828. Hugh Young, Lauriston.

Appendix III

1829. Andrew Symington, D.D., Paisley (second time).
1830. Stewart Bates, D.D., Kelso, afterwards Glasgow.
1831. Thomas Rowatt, Penpont (second time).
1832. Adam Brown, Kilmarnock (second time).
1833. William Goold, Edinburgh (second time).
1834. William Symington, D.D., Stranraer, afterwards Glasgow (second time).
1835. William Maclachlan, Kilmalcolm.
1836. James Ferguson, Kilbirnie.
1837. A. M. Rogerson, Darvel (second time).
1838. John Carslaw, Airdrie.
1839. James Macgill, Hightae.
1840 (May). Thomas Martin, Strathmiglo.
1840 (October). Joseph Henderson, Ayr.
1841. Thomas Neilson, Rothesay.
1842 (May). Malcolm M'Lachlan, Castle-Douglas.
1842 (October). John Graham, D.D., Wishaw, afterwards Ayr and Liverpool.
1843. Andrew Gilmour, Greenock.
1844. Peter Carmichael, Penpont, afterwards Greenock.
1845. John M'Kinlay, Renton, formerly O.S.
1846. Thomas Macindoe, Whithorn.
1847. John M'Dermid, Dumfries, afterwards Glasgow, Cumberland Street.
1848. William Henry Goold, D.D., Edinburgh.
1849. Andrew Symington, D.D., Paisley (third time).
1850. David Henderson, Chirnside.
1851. William Symington, Jun., D.D., Castle-Douglas.
1852. John Cunningham, LL.D., London, Missionary to the Jews.

1853. James Goold, Newton-Stewart.
1854 (January). *Pro-re-nata* as above.
1854 (May). Thomas Neilson, Rothesay (second time).
1855. John W. Macmeeken, Lesmahagow.
1856. William Anderson, Loanhead.
1857. Robert Harkness, Colmonell (resigned during office).
1858. James Ferguson, Kilbirnie (second time).
1859. James Morrison, Eskdalemuir.
1860 (May). Thomas Martin, Strathmiglo (second time).
1860 (August). William Binnie, D.D., Stirling.
1861. John Inglis, D.D., New Hebrides.
1862. Matthew George Easton, D.D., Darvel.
1863. John Graham, D.D., Liverpool (second time).
1864. John G. Paton, D.D., New Hebrides.
1865. William Maclachlan, Port Glasgow (second time).
1866. John Kay, D.D., Castle-Douglas, afterwards Coatbridge, and Edinburgh.
1867. John M'Dermid, Glasgow, Cumberland Street (second time).
1868. Charles N. M'Caig, Lochgilphead.
1869. William Symington (the younger), D.D., Glasgow, Gt. Hamilton Street (second time)
1870. George Clazy, Paisley.
1871. David Berry, Wick.
1872. John Hamilton, Renton.
1873. William H. Goold, D.D., Edinburgh, Professor (second time).

Appendix III

1874. John H. Thomson, Eaglesham, afterwards Hightae.
1875. John Torrance, Glasgow, Grant Street.
1876 (March). David Taylor, Glasgow, West Campbell Street.
1876 (May). William Henry Goold, D.D., Edinburgh (third time).

(*Union*)

Three of these Moderators were Missionaries; Drs. Inglis and Paton to the New Hebrides, and Dr. Cunningham to the Jews, the only Jewish Missionary who has occupied the Chair of the Supreme Court of any Scottish Church.

PROFESSORS.

1785. John Thorburn, Pentland, tutor, died before entering his duties.
1803. John M'Millan (*Tertius*), Stirling, died 1819.
1820. Andrew Symington, D.D., Paisley, died 1853.
1854. William Symington, D.D., Gt. Hamilton Street, Glasgow, brother of the preceding, Professor of Systematic Theology, died 1862.
1854. William Henry Goold, D.D., Edinburgh, Professor of Biblical Literature and Church History till the Union, 1876.
1862. William Binnie, D.D., Stirling, in room of Dr. Symington: became Professor of Church History in the Free Church College, Aberdeen, in 1875.

ASSOCIATE SYNOD.
MODERATORS.

[From 1733 to 1744 the Supreme Court of the Church was a Presbytery. In the latter year it was resolved to form a Synod. Ebenezer Erskine was appointed to preach a sermon appropriate to the occasion. This he did at Stirling, on 5th March 1745, and afterwards constituted the Synod by prayer. Thereafter, Ralph Erskine was chosen Moderator.]

March	1745.	Ralph Erskine, Dunfermline.
May	1745.	(*Pro-re-nata.*)
Sept.	1745.	James Thomson, Burntisland
Nov.	1745.	(*Pro-re-nata.*)
April	1746.	Alexander Moncreiff, Abernethy.
Sept.	1746.	Thomas Mair, Orwell.
April	1747.	James Mair, West Linton.

PROFESSORS OF DIVINITY.

1736. Rev. William Wilson, Perth.
1742. Rev. Alexander Moncrieff, Abernethy.

ASSOCIATE (BURGHER) SYNOD.
MODERATORS.

April	1747.	James Mair, West Linton: (continued after Breach.)
June	1747.	James Fisher, Glasgow, Greyfriars.
Sept.	1747.	Ralph Erskine, Dunfermline (second time).
Oct. 6,	1747.	(*Pro-re-nata.*)
,, 28,	1747.	(*Pro-re-nata.*)
April	1748	David Horn, Bonkle

Appendix III

May	1748.	(*Pro-re-nata.*)
Oct.	1748.	Henry Erskine, Falkirk.
Jan.	1749.	(*Pro-re-nata.*)
May	1749.	John M'Ara, Burntshields.
Sept.	1749.	William Hutton, Stow.
May	1750.	James Johnstone, Dundee, School Wynd.
July	1750.	(*Pro-re-nata.*)
Oct.	1750.	David Telfer, Bridge-of-Teith.
April	1751.	Patrick Matthew, Auchtermuchty.
May	1751.	(*Pro-re-nata.*)
July	1751.	(*Pro-re-nata.*)
Sept.	1751.	John Swanston, Kinross, West.
April	1752.	John Smith, Jedburgh, Blackfriars.
May	1752.	(*Pro-re-nata.*)
Oct.	1752.	John Jervie, Perth, Wilson Church.
May	1753.	Robert Shirra, Kirkcaldy, Bethelfield.
Nov.	1753.	John Brown, Haddington.
April	1754.	James Erskine, Stirling, Erskine Church.
Oct.	1754.	James Bennet, St. Andrews.
May	1755.	Daniel Cock, Greenock, Cartsdyke.
Sept.	1755.	John Patison, Edinburgh, Bristo.
May	1756.	William M'Ewen, Dundee, School Wynd.
Oct.	1756.	William Hutton (second time), now of Dalkeith.
April	1757.	David Horn, Bonkle (second time).
Aug.	1757.	Robert Shirra, Kirkcaldy (second time).
May	1758.	James Mair, West Linton (second time).
Oct.	1758.	John Swanston, Kinross, West (second time).
May	1759.	John M'Ara, Burntshields (second time).
Oct.	1759.	James Wylie, Scone.

Appendix III

April	1760.	David Forrest, Inverkeithing.
Aug.	1760.	John Smith, Dunfermline, Queen Anne Street.
May	1761.	Andrew Moir, Selkirk.
Oct.	1761.	George Coventry, Stitchel.
March	1762.	(*Pro-re-nata.*)
May	1762.	William Kidston. Stow.
Aug.	1762.	(*Pro-re-nata.*)
Sept.	1762.	John Belfrage, Falkirk, Erskine Church
May	1763.	John Low, Biggar.
Oct.	1763.	Archibald Hall, Torphichen.
May	1764.	Alexander Shanks, Jedburgh, Blackfriars
Oct.	1764.	William Arnot, Kennoway.
May	1765.	William Hutton, Dalkeith, Buccleuch Street (third time).
Sept.	1765.	Robert Nicol, Kelso.
Nov.	1765.	(*Pro-re-nata.*)
May	1766.	David Smith, St. Andrews.
Oct.	1766.	John Johnston, Ecclefechan.
May	1767.	William Kidston, Stow (second time)
Aug.	1767.	Robert Shirra, Kirkcaldy (third time)
May	1768.	John Jervie, Perth (second time).
Aug.	1768.	Alexander Dick, Aberdeen, Nether Kirkgate.
May	1769.	John Smith, Dunfermline (second time)
Aug.	1769.	John Henderson, Dunbar.
May	1770.	John Thomson, Kirkintilloch
Aug.	1770.	William Hall, Bathgate.
May	1771.	James Moir, Cumbernauld.
Sept.	1771.	David Walker, Pollokshaws.
May	1772.	Robert Campbell, Stirling, Erskine Ch

Appendix III

Sept.	1772.	James Scott, Musselburgh.
May	1773.	Michael Gilfillan, Dunblane.
Aug.	1773.	Samuel Kinloch, Paisley, Abbey Close
May	1774.	George Thomson, Rathillet.
Sept.	1774.	Andrew Davidson, Duns, West
March	1775.	(*Pro-re-nata.*)
May	1775.	John Riddoch, Coldstream, West.
Sept.	1775.	George Lawson, D.D., Selkirk, afterwards Professor.
May	1776.	John Marshall, Alnwick, Clayport St.
Sept.	1776.	George Henderson, Glasgow, Greyfriars
Feby.	1777.	(*Pro-re-nata.*)
May	1777.	John Belfrage, Falkirk (second time).
Sept.	1777.	William Fletcher, Bridge-of-Teith.
May	1778.	John Fraser, Auchtermuchty.
Sept.	1778.	John Morton, Leslie, Trinity.
May	1779.	Alexander Pirie, Linlithgow, West
Sept.	1779.	Thomas Porteous, Milnathort.
May	1780.	David Greig, Lochgelly.
Sept.	1780.	Andrew Dick, Queensferry.
May	1781.	Robert Shirra, Kirkcaldy (fourth time).
Sept.	1781.	John Belfrage, Falkirk (third time).
Nov.	1781.	(*Pro-re-nata.*)
May	1782.	James Scott, Musselburgh (second time).
Sept.	1782.	James Husband, D.D., Dunfermline, Queen Anne Street.
May	1783.	John Jamieson, Bathgate.
Sept.	1783.	John Young, Kincardine-on-Forth.
May	1784.	William Scott, Bonkle.
Sept.	1784.	Alexander Shanks, Jedburgh, Blackfriars (second time).

May	1785. Robert Jaffray, Kilmarnock, Portland Road.
Sept.	1785. James Hall, D.D., Cumnock, afterwards of Edinburgh.
May	1786. James M'Gilchrist, West Linton.
Sept.	1786. John Brown, Longridge.
May	1787. John Kyle, Kinross, West.
Sept.	1787. John Primrose, East Calder.
May	1788. Robert Jack, Linlithgow, West, afterwards of Greenock and Manchester, D.D.
Sept.	1788. Robert Sheriff, Tranent.
May	1789. Ebenezer Brown, Inverkeithing.
Sept.	1789. James Peddie, Edinburgh, Bristo.
May	1790. James M'Farlane, Dunfermline, Queen Anne Street.
Sept.	1790. Thomas Waters, Alloa, West.
May	1791. James Black, Dundee, School Wynd.
Sept.	1791. James Johnston, Rathillet.
May	1792. Patrick Comrie, Penicuik.
Sept.	1792. William Watson, Old Kilpatrick Craigs.
May	1793. David Hepburn, Newburgh.
Sept.	1793. William Taylor, Renton.
May	1794. David Carruthers, Queensferry.
Sept.	1794. James Hall, D.D., Edinburgh, Rose Street (second time).
May	1795. Robert Hall, Kelso (brother of the preceding).
Sept.	1795. John Dick, D.D., Slateford, afterwards of Glasgow; and Professor.
April	1796. Thomas Aitchison, Leith, Kirkgate.

Appendix III

Sept.	1796.	William Elder, Newtown, St. Boswells.
April	1797.	Alexander Black, Musselburgh, Bridge Street.
Sept.	1797.	William Willis, Greenock, Cartsdyke.
April	1798.	John Jamieson, D.D., Scone.
Sept.	1798.	George Bell, Wooler, Tower Hill.
April	1799.	Andrew Duncanson, Airdrie, Well Wynd.
Sept.	1799.	Jedidiah Aikman, Perth, Wilson Church.
April	1800.	Henry Belfrage, Falkirk, Erskine Ch.
Sept.	1800.	William Kidston, Jun., D.D., Glasgow, East Campbell Street.
April	1801.	David Wilson, Cumnock.
Sept.	1801.	James Dickson, Eaglesham.
April	1802.	George Black, Kinghorn.
Sept.	1802.	Andrew Lothian, Edinburgh, Portsburgh
April	1803.	Alexander Harper, Lanark.
Sept.	1803.	Donald Fraser, D.D., Kennoway.
April	1804.	Hugh Jamieson, D.D., East Linton.
Sept.	1804.	George Campbell, Stockbridge, Berwickshire.
April	1805.	James Dewar, Fenwick.
Sept.	1805.	Thomas Leckie, Peebles.
April	1806.	John Leech, Largs.
Sept.	1806.	Alexander Waugh, D.D., London, Albany Church.
April	1807.	William Fleming, West Calder.
Sept.	1807.	John Walker, Mauchline.
April	1808.	Thomas Brown, D.D., Dalkeith, Buccleuch Street.
Sept.	1808.	Peter Young, Jedburgh, Blackfriars.

Appendix III

April	1809.	James Keith, Fala.
Sept.	1809.	William Hadden, Limekilns.
April	1810.	James Hay, D.D., Kinross, West.
Sept.	1810.	John Richardson, Freuchie.
April	1811.	James Robertson, Wooler, Tower Hill.
Sept.	1811.	William Fraser, Alloa, West.
April	1812.	James Harrower, Denny.
Sept.	1812.	William Schaw, Ayr, Darlington Place.
April	1813.	James Law, Kirkcaldy, Bethelfield.
Sept.	1813.	David Paterson, Alnwick, Clayport Street.
April	1814.	David Telford, Buckhaven.
Sept.	1814.	James Ellis, Saltcoats, Countess Street.
April	1815.	William M'Lay, Stitchel
Sept.	1815.	Alexander O Beattie, D.D., Kincardine-on-Forth, afterwards Glasgow.
April	1816.	William Smart, Paisley, Abbey Close.
Sept.	1816.	James Blackwood, Galston.
April	1817.	John Johnston, St. Andrews.
Sept.	1817.	David Stewart, Stirling, Erskine Church
April	1818.	John M'Kerrow, D.D., Bridge-of-Teith.
Sept.	1818.	John Brown, Biggar, afterwards of Edinburgh, D.D.
April	1819.	George Young, D.D., Whitby.
Sept.	1819.	George Lawson, Kilmarnock, Portland Road.
April	1820.	Robert Balmer, D.D., Berwick, Wallace Green, afterwards Professor, continued in September.

The foregoing from Index to *Synodical Records of Burgher Synod*.

Appendix III

From 1745 to 1820, one hundred and sixty meetings of Associate Synods were held, of which—

At Edinburgh	110
At Stirling	20
At Glasgow	18
At Falkirk	7
At Dunfermline	5
	160

PROFESSORS OF DIVINITY.

1747. Ebenezer Erskine, Stirling.
1749. James Fisher, Glasgow.
1764. John Swanston, Kinross.
1768. John Brown, Haddington.
1787. George Lawson, D.D., Selkirk.

GENERAL ASSOCIATE SYNOD.
(ANTI-BURGHER.)
MODERATORS.

['In Mr. Gib's house, 10th April 1747, which day and place the Associate Synod being met and constituted with prayer by the Rev. Mr. Thomas Mair, who, as last Moderator, opened the meeting of Synod on Tuesday, this week, with a sermon from Judges xiii. 9, "And the angel . . . Be still and know that I am God . . ."

'Mr. Thomas Mair was unanimously continued in the chair. Mr. Gib, clerk, *pro tem.*']

Aug. 1747. James Thomson, Burntisland.
Nov. 1747. (*Pro-re-nata.*)

Appendix III

Jany. 1748. (*Pro-re-nata.*)
April 1748. Alexander Moncrieff, Abernethy.
Aug. 1748. Adam Gib, Edinburgh.
Jany. 1749. (*Pro-re-nata.*)
April 1749. David Smyton, Kilmaurs.
Aug. 1749. George Brown, Perth, North.
Feby. 1750. William Campbell, Ceres, West.
Aug. 1750. Andrew Clarkson, Linlithgow, Craigmailen.
Feby. 1751. James Scot, Morebattle.
Aug. 1751. Andrew Thomson, Mearns.
Feby. 1752. William Mair, Muckart.
Aug. 1752. John Whyte, Duns, East.
April 1753. John Muckersie, Kinkell.
Oct. 1753. George Murray, *Primus*, Lockerbie.
April 1754. Alexander Blyth, Kinclaven.
Aug. 1754. Robert Archibald, Haddington.
March 1755. William Moncrieff, Alloa, Townhead.
Aug. 1755. Matthew Moncrieff, Abernethy, brother of preceding.
April 1756. John Goodlet, Sanquhar, South
Aug. 1756. John Walker, Dennyloanhead.
April 1757. Andrew Arnot, Midholm.
Aug. 1757. John Dalziell, Earlston, East.
March 1758. John Jamieson, Glasgow, Cathedral Sq.
Aug. 1758. John Heugh, Stirling, Viewfield.
April 1759. John Wilson, Methven.
Oct. 1759. James Mitchell, Holm of Balfron.
April 1760. Andrew Bunyan, Howgate.
Aug. 1760. Richard Jerment, Peebles.
April 1761. William Oliver, Hamilton, Saffronhall.

Appendix III

Aug.	1761.	John Robertson, Dalkeith, Back Street.
April	1762.	James Morison, Norham.
Aug.	1762.	James Burt, Cairneyhill.
April	1763.	Thomas Thomson, Kirkcaldy, Pathhead.
Aug.	1763.	Alexander Troup, Elgin, South Street.
April	1764.	Alexander Preston, Logiealmond.
Sept.	1764.	Josiah Hunter, Falkirk.
April	1765.	James Alice, Paisley, Oakshaw Street.
Sept.	1765.	William Moncrieff, Alloa (second time).
April	1766.	James Scot, Morebattle (second time).
Aug. 26.	1766.	John Goodlet, Sanquhar, South (second time).
April	1767.	John Dalziell, Earlstoun, East (second time).
Sept.	1767.	John Buist, Greenock, Greenbank.
April	1768.	John Wilson, Methven (second time).
Aug.	1768.	John Walker, Dennyloanhead (second time).
	1769.	William Graham, Whitehaven, afterwards of Newcastle.
May	1770.	Andrew Thomson, Mearns (second time).
Oct.	1770.	Robert Cunningham, Eastbarns, Dunbar.
April	1771.	George Murray, *Secundus*, Lockerbie.
Aug.	1771.	John Heugh, Stirling (second time).
April	1772.	William Oliver, Hamilton (second time).
Sept.	1772.	Andrew Bunyan, Howgate (second time).
May	1773.	James Mitchell, Balfron (second time)

Appendix III

Aug.	1773.	Laurence Wotherspoon, Haddington.
May	1774.	John Robertson, Jedburgh, Castle Street.
Aug.	1774.	Thomas Thomson, Kirkcaldy, Pathhead (second time).
May	1775.	James Alice, Paisley (second time).
Aug.	1775.	John Anderson, Elsridgehill.
April	1776.	Thomas Bennet, Ceres.
Sept.	1776.	William M'George, Mid-Calder.
April	1777.	William Jameson, Kilwinning.
Aug.	1777.	James Henderson, Rattray.
April	1778.	Archibald Bruce, Whitburn.
Aug.	1778.	Michael Arthur, Peebles.
April	1779.	Colin Brown, Abernethy.
Aug.	1779.	John Young, Orrock Place, Hawick.
May	1780.	William Inglis, Dumfries, Loreburn Street.
Aug.	1780.	James Russell, Milnathort.
May	1781.	John Muckersie, Kinkell (second time).
Aug.	1781.	James Ramsay, Glasgow, Cathedral Square.
April	1782.	John Gray, Brechin, City Road.
Sept.	1782.	Andrew Arnot, Midholm (second time).
May	1783.	Alexander Pringle, D.D., Perth, North.
Sept.	1783.	Thomas Russell, Greenloaning.
May	1784.	John Turnbull, Ayton.
Aug.	1784.	George Whytock, Dalkeith, Back Street.
April	1785.	James Aitken, Kirriemuir.
Aug.	1785.	James Robertson, Kilmarnock, Clerk's Lane.
May	1786.	Thomas Cleland, Bo'ness.

Appendix III

Sept.	1786.	David Sommerville, Strathaven, first.
	1787.	John Jamieson, D.D., Forfar, afterwards Edinburgh.
	1788.	James Morison, Norham (second time).
April	1789.	John Robertson, Jedburgh, Castle Street (second time).
Sept.	1789.	Robert Cunningham, Eastbarns, Dunbar (second time).
April	1790.	John Young, Hawick (second time).
Sept.	1790.	Robert Laing, Duns, East.
May	1791.	John Gray, Brechin, City Road (second time).
Aug.	1791.	David Morrison, Morebattle.
April	1792.	John Heugh, Stirling (third time).
Aug.	1792.	Robert Colville, Lauder.
April	1793.	James M'Ewan, Bell Street, Dundee.
Sept.	1793.	Andrew Arnot, Midholm (third time).
April	1794.	James Hog, Kelso.
Sept.	1794.	Andrew Bunyan, Howgate (third time), died in office.
April	1795.	Alexander Allan, Coupar-Angus.
	(1796-1798 awanting.)	
April	1799.	Andrew Imrie, Milnathort.
Sept.	1799.	Thomas M'Crie, D.D., Edinburgh, Potterrow.
April	1800.	Robert Imrie, Kinkell.
Sept.	1800.	Alexander Moncrieff, Muckart.
April	1801.	James Hay, Alyth.
Oct.	1801.	Andrew Mitchell, Beith.
April	1802.	David Ross, Burntisland.
Aug.	1802.	Alexander Oliver, Craigmailen.

	1803. William Ferrier, D.D., Paisley, Oakshaw Street.
	1804. Richard Black, Perth, North.
	1805. William Drysdale, Stranraer, Ivy Place.
April	1806. George Jerment, D.D., London, Oxendon.
Aug.	1806. John Mitchell, D.D., Glasgow, Wellington Street.
	1807. James Brownlee, Falkirk, Graham's Road.
April	1808. Andrew Thomson, Sanquhar, South.
Aug	1808. James Stark, Dennyloanhead.
	1809. George Stevenson, D.D., Ayr.
	1810. John Nicholson, Belfast.
April	1811. David Waddell, Shiels.
Aug.	1811. John Murray, Carnoustie.
	1812. David Meek, Muirton.
	1813. John Jameson, Methven.
	1814. James Muckersie, Alloa, Townhead.
May	1815. Robert Muter, D.D., Glasgow, Duke Street.
Oct.	1815. George Paxton, D.D., Professor.
	1816. John Robertson, Stranraer, Ivy Place.
	1817. James Pringle, Newcastle, Westmoreland Road.
May	1818. William M'Ewen, Howgate.
Oct.	1818. James Templeton, Aberdeen, Belmont Street.
May	1819. Hugh Heugh, Stirling, Viewfield.
Sept.	1819. Alexander Young, Logiealmond.

Appendix III

April 1820. William Broadfoot, London, Oxendon Street.
Sept. 1820. John Jamieson, D.D., Edinburgh, Nicolson Street (second time).

[The foregoing from Scroll Minutes I. to VI.]

PROFESSORS

1747. Alexander Moncrieff, Abernethy.
1762. William Moncrieff, Alloa.
1786. Archibald Bruce, Whitburn.
1807. George Paxton, D.D., Edinburgh.

UNITED SECESSION SYNOD.
MODERATORS.

Sept. 1820. David Greig, Lochgelly.
April 1821. Alexander Pringle, D.D., Perth, North.
Sept. 1821. Jas. Hall, D.D., Edinburgh, Broughton Place.
April 1822. John Jamieson, D.D., Edinburgh, Nicolson Street.
Sept. 1822. John Brown, Longridge.
April 1823. William Ferrier, D.D., Paisley, Oakshaw Street.
Sept. 1823. James Stark, Dennyloanhead.
April 1824. Henry Belfrage, D.D., Falkirk, Erskine Church.
Sept. 1824. James Hay, Alyth.
May 1825. James Peddie, D.D., Edinburgh, Bristo.
Sept. 1825. John Mitchell, D.D., Glasgow, Wellington Street.

April	1826.	John Dick, D.D., Glasgow, Greyfriars.
Sept.	1826.	Robert Muter, D.D., Glasgow, Duke Street.
May	1827.	James Hay, D.D., Kinross, West.
Sept.	1827.	Alexander Duncan, D.D., Mid-Calder.
May	1828.	James Ellis, Saltcoats, Countess Street.
Sept.	1828.	Andrew Lothian, Edinburgh, Portsburgh
April	1829.	Hugh Heugh, D.D., Glasgow, Regent Place.
Sept.	1829.	John Brown, D.D., Edin., Broughton Place.
April	1830.	William Kidston, D.D , Glasgow, East Campbell Street.
Sept.	1830.	John Ritchie. D.D., Edinburgh, Potterrow.
April	1831.	Donald Fraser, D.D., Kennoway.
Sept.	1831.	David Young, D.D., Perth, North.
April	1832.	George Lawson, Kilmarnock, Portland Road.
Sept.	1832.	James Clark, Jedburgh, Castle Street.
April	1833.	William Smart, Paisley, Abbey Close.
Sept.	1833.	Alexander O. Beattie, M.D., D.D., Glasgow, Gordon Street.
April	1834.	James Pringle, Newcastle, Westmoreland Road.
Sept.	1834.	John Clapperton, Johnstone, West.
April	1835.	David Ronald, Saltcoats, West.
Sept.	1835.	Adam Thomson, D.D., Coldstream, West.
April	1836.	David Wilson, Kilmarnock, Clerk's Lane.
Sept.	1836.	Alexander Campbell, Irvine, Trinity.

Appendix III

May	1837.	Andrew Marshall, D.D., LL.D., Kirkintilloch.
Sept.	1837.	William Schaw, D.D., Ayr, Darlington Place.
Jany.	1838.	William Schaw, D.D., Ayr, Darlington Place (second time).
May	1838.	Robert Paterson, D.D., Kirkwall.
June	1839.	John M'Kerrow, D.D., Bridge-of-Teith.
June	1840.	James Harper, D.D., Leith, North.
June	1841.	Archibald Baird, D.D., Paisley, St. James.
May	1842.	John Smart, D.D., Leith, St. Andrew's Place.
May	1843.	Andrew Elliot, Ford.
Oct.	1843.	Thomas Struthers, Hamilton, Avon Street.
May	1844.	Thomas Stark, Forres.
May	1845.	William Fleming, West Calder.
July	1845.	Joseph Hay, Arbroath, Princes Street.
May	1846.	John Lamb, Errol.
Oct.	1846,	John Newlands, D.D., Perth, Wilson Church; continued to May 1847.

The Rev. Messrs. Greig, Brown, Hay of Kinross, Ellis, Lothian, Lawson, William Smart, and Fleming; and Drs. Hall, Belfrage, Peddie, Dick, Brown, Kidston, Fraser, Beattie, Schaw, and M'Kerrow were previously Moderators of the Burgher Synod. Messrs. Stark, Hay (Alyth), and Pringle; and Drs. Jamieson, Ferrier, Mitchell, Muter, and Heugh were Moderators of the Anti-Burgher Synod. It will be noticed that two Browns, father and son, were both

Moderators of the Burgher and United Secession Synods. The father of the elder one, the well-known John Brown of Haddington, was also Moderator of the Burgher Synod, three descents.

PROFESSORS.

1820. John Dick, D.D., Glasgow, died 1833.
1825. John Mitchell, D.D., Glasgow, Biblical Literature, resigned 1843.
1834. John Brown, D.D., Edinburgh, Exegetical Theology, till Union.
1834. Alexander Duncan, D.D., Mid-Calder, Pastoral Theology and Church History, retired 1843.
1834. Robert Balmer, D.D., Berwick, Systematic Theology, died 1844.
1843. James Harper, D.D., Leith, Pastoral Theology, till Union.
1843. John Eadie, D.D , Glasgow, Biblical Literature, till Union.

ORIGINAL ASSOCIATE SYNOD
(OLD LIGHT BURGHERS.)
[Formed 3rd September 1805.]
MODERATORS.

	1805.	Thomas Porteous, Orwell or Milnathort.
May	1806.	Ebenezer Hislop, Shotts.
Sept.	1806.	William Willis, Stirling.
April	1807.	George Hill, Cumbernauld.
Sept.	1807.	William Taylor, Perth.
April	1808.	Robert Shirra, Yetholm.

Appendix III

Sept.	1808.	Patrick Connel, Bathgate.
	1809.	Alexander Brown, Burntshields
	1810.	James Gardner, Kilpatrick.
	1811.	George Moscrip, Greenock.
	1812.	John Inglis, Greenlaw.
	1813.	William Raeburn, Bannockburn.
	1814.	Finlay Stewart, Pollokshaws.
	1815.	Robert Torrance, Airdrie.
April	1816.	William Primrose, Aberdeen.
Sept.	1816.	Alexander Stark, Falkirk.
April	1817.	Samuel Armour, Doune.
Sept.	1817.	(*Pro-re-nata*) Samuel Armour, Doune
April	1818.	James Smith, Alloa.
July	1818.	(*Pro-re-nata*) James Smith, Alloa.
May	1819.	John Mackinlay, Renton.
Sept.	1819.	Alexander Turnbull, Glasgow
	1820.	Robert Aitken, Dundee.
May	1821.	James Thornton, Milnathort.

May 15, 1821. (*In hunc effectum*) Finlay Stewart, *pro tem.*

	1822.	William Dalziel, Dunfermline.
May	1823.	Peter Campbell, Kilmarnock.

May 27, 1823. (*In hunc effectum*) William Raeburn, *pro tem.*

May	1824.	John Shaw, Boardmills.
Sept.	1824.	William Logan, Lesmahagow.
	1825.	Peter Currie, Cumbernauld.
	1826.	William Stewart, Garvagh, Ireland.
May	1827.	Thomas Hislop, Doune.
Oct.	1827.	George Hill, Shottsburn.
	1828.	Ebenezer Anderson, Cupar-Fife.

	1829. James Anderson, Carluke
	1830. Michael Willis, D.D., LL.D., Renfield Street, Glasgow.
	1831. Thomas Gordon, Falkirk.
	1832. William Scott Hay, Burntshields
May	1833. Andrew Thomson, Paisley.
Oct.	1833. David Headrick, Longridge.
May	1834. William Mackray, Stirling.
Sept.	1834. James Duncan, Kincardine-on-Forth.
May	1835. Ralph Robb, Strathkinnes.
Sept.	1835. John Waddell, Burrelton.
May	1836. John Anderson, Helensburgh.
Oct.	1836. William Tannahill, Kirkintilloch.
May	1837 George Moscrip, Greenock (second time).
Sept.	1837. John Cochrane, Cumbernauld.
	1838. James Clelland, Stewarton.
May	1839. Robert M'Indoe, Kirkcaldy.
July	1839. John Wright, Alloa.

Professors.

1800. William Willis, Greenock, resigned 1803.
1803. George Hill, Cumbernauld, died 1819.
1818. William Taylor, Perth, resigned 1833.
1835. Michael Willis, D.D., LL.D., Glasgow, till the Union, 1839.

Remanent Synod.

Aug.	1839. (*Committee*) Finlay Stewart, Pollokshaws
Sept.	1839. Finlay Stewart, Pollokshaws (second time).
June	1840. John Downs, Boardmills

Appendix III 239

Dec. 1840. (*Pro-re-nata*) John Downs, Boardmills.
April 1841. (*Pro-re-nata*) John M'Kinlay, *pro tem*
June 1841. John M'Kinlay, Renton (second time), afterwards R.P.
Nov. 1841. John Hastie, Yetholm.
Dec. 1841. John M'Kinlay, Glasgow, *pro tem.*
April 1842. John Hastie, Yetholm (second time)
May 1842. Adam Ross, Kennoway.

Messrs. Porteous, Willis and Taylor were both Moderators of the Burgher Synod before the Separation. Mr. M'Kinlay was afterwards Moderator of the Reformed Presbyterian Synod.

SYNOD OF PROTESTERS

MODERATORS.

May 1821. Richard Black, Perth.
Sept. 1821. George Paxton, D.D., Edinburgh.
May 1822. James Gray, Brechin.
Sept. 1822. Robert Smith, Kilwinning.
May 1823. George Stevenson, D.D., Ayr.
Oct. 1823. William Beath, Pitcairngreen.
May 1824. James Templeton, Aberdeen.
Oct. 1824. Thomas Gray, Kirkcaldy.
May 1825. Peter M'Derment, Auchinleck.
Sept. 1825. George Paxton, D.D., Edinburgh (second time).
May 1826. Jas. Gray, Brechin (second time).
Nov. 1826. Robert Smith, Kilwinning (second time).

May 1827. George Stevenson, D.D., Ayr (second time).

[All the meetings were held in Edinburgh.

The Rev. Richard Black, and Drs. Paxton and Stevenson were Moderators of the Anti-Burgher Synod before the Separation.]

ORIGINAL SECESSION SYNOD.

MODERATORS.

May	1827.	James Aitken, Kirriemuir.
Oct.	1827.	Professor Paxton, D.D., Edinburgh (third time).
May	1828.	Robert Chalmers, Haddington.
Sept.	1828.	James Gray, Brechin (third time).
May	1829.	Thomas M'Crie, D.D., Edinburgh.
Sept.	1829.	George Stevenson, D.D., Ayr (third time).
	1830.	Robert Smith, Kilwinning (third time).
	1831.	Thomas Gray, Kirkcaldy (second time).
	1832.	John Aitken, Aberdeen.
	1833.	Robert Shaw, D.D., Whitburn.
May	1834.	Alexander Duncan, Dundee.
Sept.	1834.	Thomas Manson, Perth.
	1835.	Thomas M'Crie, D.D., Clola.
	1836.	Benjamin Laing, D.D., Colmonell.
May	1837.	James Beattie, Balmullo.
Sept.	1837.	Matthew Murray, D.D., Glasgow.
	1838.	James Meek, Carnoustie.
	1839.	James Cairncross, Birsay.

May	1840.	George Stevenson, D.D., Ayr (fourth time).
Aug.	1840.	James Wright, Edinburgh.
April	1841.	David Sturrock, Midholm.
Sept.	1841.	Archibald Brown, Kirriemuir.
Jany.	1842.	James A. Wylie, Dollar.

UNITED ORIGINAL SECESSION SYNOD.
MODERATORS.

May	1842.	James Gray, Brechin (fourth time), and James Anderson, Carluke, as Assistant.
Sept.	1842.	(*Pro-re-nata*) as above.
May	1843.	James Anderson, Carluke.
Aug.	1843.	George Hill, Shottsburn (second time).
	1844.	John Sandison, Arbroath.
April	1845.	Robert John Watt, Stranraer.
Aug.	1845.	Thomas Manson, Perth.
	1846.	William Tannahill, Kirkintilloch (second time), died in office.
April	1847.	John Aitken, Aberdeen (second time).
July	1847.	(*Pro-re-nata*) as above.
May	1848.	James Black, Kirkcaldy.
Oct.	1848.	(*Pro-re-nata*) as above.
	1849.	George M'Crie, Clola.
April	1850.	James Meek, Carnoustie (second time).
Nov.	1850.	(*Pro-re-nata*) as above.
	1851.	John Miller, Toberdoney.
April	1852.	David Burn, Thurso.

May 1852. Thomas M'Crie, D.D., Edinburgh (second time).

Rev. Thomas M'Crie, D.D., Sen., was Moderator of the Anti-Burgher Synod before the Separation, and James Anderson, Carluke, of the Associate Burgher Synod.

PROFESSORS (ANTI-BURGHER AND ORIGINAL SECESSION.)

1786. Archibald Bruce, Whitburn, died 1816.
1807. George Paxton, D.D, Edinburgh, resigned 1836.
1836. Thomas M'Crie, D.D., LL.D., Edinburgh, till the Union.
1839. Benjamin Laing, B.D., Colmonell, till the Union.

RELIEF SYNOD.

MODERATORS.

James Baine, Edinburgh, opened with a sermon.

1773. Thomas Scott, Auchtermuchty, West.
1774. Alexander Simpson, D.D., Bellshill.
1775. Michael Boston, Falkirk, West.
1776. James Pinkerton, Campbeltown.
1777. Thomas Bell, Jedburgh, High Street.
1778. John Kerr, Bellshill.
1779. Laurence Bonar, Cupar-Fife, Boston Church.
1780. Patrick Hutchison, St. Ninians.
1781. Robert Paterson, Largo.
1782. Andrew Thomson, Berwick, Chapel Street.
1783. George H. Nicholson, Wamphray.

Appendix III 243

1784. James Stewart, Anderston, Glasgow.
1785. Joseph Johnston, Kinghorn.
1786. William Wright, Ford.
1787. James Scott, Jedburgh, High Street.
1788. John Lawson, Dumfries, Townhead.
1789. Thomas Bell, Glasgow, Cathedral Street (second time).
1790. Thomas Thomson, Duns, South.
1791. James Dun, Kilsyth.
1792. John King, Kettle.
1793. Neil Douglas, Dundee, West Port.
1794. Archibald Murdoch, Kilmaronock.
1795. William Billerwell, Dysart.
1796. William M'Kechney, Musselburgh, Mill Hill.
1797. Archibald Cross, St. Ninians.
1798. James Struthers, Edinburgh, College Street.
1799. John Pitcairn, Kelso, East.
1800. James Bonnar, Auchtermuchty, West.
1801. John Brodie, Glasgow, Cathedral Street.
1802. James Stewart, Glasgow, Anderston (second time).
1803. James Pinkerton, Campbeltown (second time).
1804. David Fergus, Auchterarder.
1805. John Reston, Edinburgh, Carrubbers' Close.
1806. John Watson, Glasgow, John Street.
1807. William Thomson, Glasgow, Hutchesontown.
1808. Robert Walker, Cupar-Fife, Boston.
1809. John Fergus, East Kilbride.
1810. John Kirkwood, Strathaven, East.
1811. James Smith, Edinburgh, College Street.
1812. James Logan, St. Ninians.

Appendix III

1813. William Carrick, Hamilton, Auchingramont.
1814. Daniel M'Naught, Biggar, Gillespie.
1815. Edward Dobbie, Burnhead, Penpont.
1816. John M'Dermid, Paisley, Canal Street.
1817. James Thomson, Paisley, Thread Street.
1818. John Ralston, Duns, South.
1819. William M'Ilquham, Tollcross, Glasgow.
1820. Henry Paterson, Gateside, Wamphray.
1821. William Auld, Greenock, Sir Michael Street.
1822. John Johnston, Edinburgh, Roxburgh Place.
1823. John M'Farlane, Glasgow, Greenhead.
1824. James Scott, Edinburgh, Bread Street.
1825. James Anderson, Beith.
1826. William Dunn, Coupar-Angus.
1827. John Anderson, Kilsyth.
1828. James Kirkwood, Edinburgh, St. James Place.
1829. Robert Brodie, Glasgow, East Campbell Street.
1830. Gavin Struthers, D.D., Glasgow, Anderston.
1831. Alexander M'Naughton, Milngavie.
1832. David Crawford, D.D., Earlstoun, West.
1833. John French, D.D., Edinburgh, College Street.
1834. William Welsh, Falkirk, West.
1835. William Anderson, LL.D., Glasgow, John Street.
1836. Matthew Allison, Kilbarchan.
1837. Alexander Harvey, Glasgow, Calton.
1838. Daniel Gorrie, Kettle.
1839. William M'Dougall, Paisley, Thread Street.
1840. James Porteous, Coldstream, East.
1841. Francis Muir, Leith, Junction Road.

Appendix III 245

	1842.	John M'Gregor, Stranraer, Bridge Street.
	1843.	Peter Brown, Wishaw.
	1844.	Robert Renwick, Ayr, Cathcart Street.
	1845.	James S. Taylor, Glasgow, Hutchesontown.
May	1846.	James Reston, Dundee, James' Church.
Oct.	1846.	W. A. Pettigrew, Dysart.
	1847.	William Auld, Greenock, Sir Michael Street (second time).

PROFESSORS.

1824. James Thomson, D.D., Paisley, died 1841.
1841. William Lindsay, D.D., Cathedral Street, Glasgow, till Union.
1841. Neil M'Michael, D.D., Dunfermline, till Union.

The Relief Synod met in Edinburgh from 1773 till 1790. Afterwards twenty-four meetings were held in Glasgow and thirty-four in Edinburgh, after which the Union with the Secession took place.

UNITED PRESBYTERIAN SYNOD.

MODERATORS from 1847 to 1900.

1847. William Kidston, D.D., Glasgow, East Campbell Street.
1847. James Kirkwood, Edinburgh, James' Place.
1848. Gavin Struthers, D.D., Glasgow, Anderston.
1849. James Meikle, D.D., Beith, Mitchell Street.
1850. Henry Angus, Aberdeen, St. Nicholas.

1851. William Lindsay, D.D., Glasgow, Cathedral Street.
1852. Henry Renton, Kelso, Trinity.
1853. George Johnston, D.D., Edinburgh, Nicolson Street.
1854. William Johnston, D.D., Limekilns.
1855. Neil M'Michael, D.D., Dunfermline, Gillespie Church.
1856. William M'Kelvie, D.D., Balgedie.
1857. John Eadie, LL.D., D.D., Glasgow, Cambridge Street.
1858. William Peddie, D.D., Edinburgh, Bristo.
1859. James Boyd, D.D., Campbeltown, Longrow.
1860. James Harper, D.D., Leith, North.
1861. John Robson, D.D., Glasgow, Wellington Street.
1862. David Smith, D.D., Biggar, Moat Park.
1863. Alexander Young, Logiealmond.
1864. David King, LL.D., London, Westbourne Grove.
1865. William Marshall, D.D., Coupar-Angus, South.
1866. John Macfarlane, LL.D., London, Clapham Road.
1867. Thomas Finlayson, D.D., Edinburgh, Rose Street.
*1868. Robert Frew, D.D., St. Ninians.
1869. William Bruce, D.D., Edinburgh, Infirmary Street.
1870. Peter M'Dowall, Alloa, Townhead.
1871. John Edmond, D.D., London, Highbury.

Appendix III

1872. John Cairns, D.D., Berwick, Wallace Green.
1873. Joseph Brown, D.D., Glasgow, Kent Road.
1874. Andrew Thomson, D.D., Edinburgh, Broughton Place.
1875. James R. M'Gavin, D.D., Dundee, Tay Square.
1876. John Rankine, Cupar-Fife, Bonnygate.
1877. William France, Paisley, Oakshaw Street.
1878. David M. Croom, Edinburgh, Lauriston Place.
1879. George Jeffrey, D.D., Glasgow, London Road.
1880. Henry Calderwood, LL.D., Edinburgh, Professor of Moral Philosophy.
1881. John Clark, Abernethy.
1882. David Young, D.D., Glasgow, Woodlands Road.
1883. Robert S. Scott, D.D., Glasgow, Home Secretary.
*1884. George C. Hutton, D.D., Paisley, Canal Street.
1885. John Logan Aikman, D.D., Glasgow, Anderston (died in office).
1886. David Duff, D.D.,LL.D., Edinburgh, Professor
1887. John B. Smith, Greenock, Union Street.
1888. Williamson Shoolbred, D.D., Beawr, India.
*1889. Robert S. Drummond, D.D., Glasgow, Belhaven Church.
1890. James Fleming, Whithorn.
1891. Andrew Henderson, LL.D., Paisley, Abbey Close.
*1892. James Black, D.D., Glasgow, Wellington Street.

Appendix III

*1893. Thomas Kennedy, D.D., Edinburgh, North Richmond Street.
*1894. Alexander Oliver, D.D., Glasgow, Regent Place.
 1895. David Kinnear, Dalbeattie.
*1896. James Rennie, Glasgow, St. Vincent Street.
 1897. John Hutchison, D.D., Leith, Bonnington.
*1898. William Blair, D.D., Dunblane.
*1899. John Robson, D.D., Aberdeen, St. Nicholas.
*1900. Alexander Mair, D.D., Edinburgh, Morningside. (*Annual and Union Synods.*)

The Synods of 1854 and 1877 were held in Glasgow. The others met in Edinburgh: that of May 1847 in Tanfield Hall and Bristo Church, that of October 1847 in Bristo Church; those of 1848-53, 1855-76, and 1878 in the Synod Hall, Queen Street; that of 1879 in the Free Assembly Hall on the Mound; the remainder in the Synod Hall, Castle Terrace. Dr. Kidston had previously been Moderator of the Burgher and the United Secession Synods; Mr. Kirkwood and Dr. Struthers of the Relief Synod; Dr. Harper of the United Secession Synod, and Mr. Young of the Anti-Burgher. The last-named, when Moderator in 1863, was the oldest minister on active duty in Scotland; the only one ordained before him, living in that year, bore the same name, Mr. Young, Parish Minister of Wigtown. Of the Moderators, 11 were connected with Edinburgh, 13 with Glasgow, 16 with other towns, 9 with rural districts, and 1 with the foreign field;

Appendix III

7 were Principals or Professors, and Dr. Calderwood was a University Professor. Names marked by an asterisk are those of ministers still living (1906).

PROFESSORS.

John Brown, D.D., Edinburgh, Exegetical Theology, 1847-58.

William Lindsay, D.D., Glasgow, Oriental Languages, 1847-66.

James Harper, D.D., Leith, Systematic Theology, 1847-79.

Neil M'Michael, D.D., Church History, Dunfermline, 1847-74.

John Eadie, D.D., LL.D., Glasgow, Exegetical Theology, 1847-76.

John Cairns, D.D., Berwick, Apologetics, 1867-92.

Robert Johnstone, D.D., Exegetical Theology, 1876 till Union.

James A. Paterson, D.D., Hebrew, 1876 till Union.

David Duff, D.D., Church History, 1876-90.

John Ker, D.D., Practical Training, 1876-86.

James Orr, D.D., Church History, 1891 till Union.

James Wardrop, D.D., Systematic Theology, etc., 1892 till Union.

Alexander Hislop, D.D., Practical Training, 1892 till Union.

PRINCIPALS.

1876. James Harper, D.D.
1879. John Cairns, D.D.
1892. George C. Hutton, D.D.

Appendix III

FREE CHURCH OF SCOTLAND.
MODERATORS from 1843 to 1900.

May	1843. Thomas Chalmers, D.D., LL.D., D.C.L., Edinburgh, Principal.
Oct.	1843. Thomas Brown, D.D., Glasgow, St. John's.
	1844. Henry Grey, D.D., Edinburgh, St. Mary's.
May	1845. Patrick M'Farlan, D.D., Greenock, West.
Aug.	1845. Same as above.
	1846. Robert James Brown, D.D., Aberdeen, Professor of Greek, Marischal College.
	1847. James Sieveright, D.D., Markinch.
	1848. Patrick Clason, D.D., Edinburgh, Buccleuch.
	1849. Mackintosh Mackay, LL.D., Dunoon.
	1850. Nathaniel Paterson, D.D., Glasgow, St. Andrew's.
	1851. Alexander Duff, D.D., LL.D., Calcutta.
	1852. Angus Mackellar, D.D., Edinburgh, Ret.
	1853. John Smyth, D.D., Glasgow, St. George's.
	1854. James Grierson, D.D., Errol.
	1855. James Henderson, D.D., Glasgow, St. Enoch's.
	1856. Thomas M'Crie, D.D., LL.D., M'Crie Church, appointed Professor in the English Presbyterian College, London, the same year.
	1857. James J. Wood, D.D., Dumfries, St. George's.

Appendix III

1858. Alexander Beith, D.D., Stirling, North.
1859. William Cunningham, D.D., Edinburgh, Principal.
1860. Robert Buchanan, D.D., Glasgow, College Church.
1861. Robert S. Candlish, D.D., Edinburgh, St. George's; afterwards Principal, New College.
1862. Thomas Guthrie, D.D., Edinburgh, St. John's.
1863. Roderick M'Leod, Snizort.
1864. Patrick Fairbairn, D.D., Glasgow, Principal.
1865. James Begg, D.D., Edinburgh, Newington.
1866. William Wilson, D.D., Dundee, St. Paul's.
1867. John Roxburgh, D.D., Glasgow, St. John's.
1868. William Nixon, D.D., Montrose, St. John's.
1869. Sir Henry W. Moncreiff, Bart., D.D., Edinburgh, St. Cuthbert's.
1870. John Wilson, D.D., Bombay.
1871. Robert Elder, D.D., Rothesay, West.
1872. Charles J. Brown, D.D., Edinburgh, New North.
1873. Alexander Duff, D.D., LL.D., Edinburgh, Professor (second time).
1874. Robert W. Stewart, D.D., Leghorn.
1875. Alexander Moody Stuart D.D., Edinburgh, St. Luke's.
1876. Thomas M'Lauchlan, LL.D., Edinburgh, St. Columba.
1877. William Henry Goold, D.D., Edinburgh, Martyr's.
1878. Andrew A. Bonar, D.D., Glasgow, Finnieston.

Appendix III

1879. James C. Burns, D.D., Kirkliston.
1880. Thomas Main, D.D., Edinburgh, St. Mary's.
1881. William Laughton, D.D., Greenock, St. Thomas.
1882. Robert M'Donald, D.D., Leith, North.
1883. Horatius Bonar, D.D., Edinburgh, Grange.
1884. Walter R. Taylor, D.D., Thurso, First.
1885. David Brown, D.D., Aberdeen, Principal.
1886. Alexander N. Sommerville, D.D., Glasgow, Anderston.
*1887. Robert Rainy, D.D., Edinburgh, Principal.
1888. Gustavus Aird, D.D., Creich.
1889. John Laird, D.D., Cupar.
1890. Thomas Brown, D.D., Edinburgh, Dean.
*1891. Thomas Smith, D.D., LL.D., Edinburgh, Professor.
1892. William G. Blaikie, D.D., LL.D., Edinburgh, Professor.
*1893. Walter C. Smith, D.D., LL.D., Edinburgh, High.
1894. George C. M. Douglas, D.D., Glasgow, Principal.
1895. James H. Wilson, D.D., Edinburgh, Barclay.
*1896. William Miller, C.I.E., D.D., LL.D., Madras.
1897. Hugh Macmillan, D.D., LL.D., Greenock, West.
*1898. Alexander Whyte, D.D., Edinburgh, St. George's.
1899. James Stewart, M.D., D.D., Lovedale.
*1900. Walter Ross Taylor, D.D., Glasgow, Kelvinside. (*Annual and Union Assemblies.*)

Appendix III

PRINCIPAL CLERKS OF ASSEMBLY.

Thomas Pitcairn, Cockpen, 1843-1854.
Patrick Clason, D.D., Edinburgh, 1843-1867.
Sir H. W. Moncreiff, Bart., D.D., Edinburgh, 1855-1883.
William Wilson, D.D., Dundee, 1868-1888.
Andrew Melville, D.D., Glasgow, 1884 till Union.
Archibald Henderson, D.D., Crieff, 1888 till Union.

DEPUTE CLERKS.

1843. James Crawford, W.S.
1864. George Meldrum, C.A.
1877. Robert R. Simpson, W.S.

The Assembly of October 1843, and that of 1878 were held in Glasgow, those of August 1845, and of 1888, in Inverness. The rest met in Edinburgh, those from 1843 to 1855 in Tanfield Hall, those of the three following years, in the Music Hall, and those from 1859 till 1900, in the Assembly Hall on the Mound. Drs. Chalmers, M'Farlane, and Mackellar had been Moderators of the unbroken Church, Dr. M'Crie of the Original Secession Synod, Dr. Goold of the Reformed Presbyterian Synod, and Dr. Burns of the English Presbyterian Synod. Drs. Duff, John Wilson, Thomas Smith, Miller, and James Stewart had been Missionaries in the Foreign Field. Dr. Robert W. Stewart laboured in the Continental field. Drs. Duff and Thomas Smith were also Professors in the New College, Edinburgh. Four Moderators were Principals, and one a Professor in

Edinburgh, two were Principals in Glasgow, and one held the same office in Aberdeen. Another was a Professor in Marischal College, Aberdeen; of the remaining forty-three, seventeen were connected with Edinburgh, nine with Glasgow, eleven with other towns, and only five with rural districts, two in the Highlands, three in the Lowlands. Two pairs of brothers occupied the chair, Drs. Charles and David Brown, and Drs. Andrew and Horatius Bonar; also a father and a son, Drs. Taylor of Thurso and Glasgow. Those marked by asterisks are still living (1906).

PRINCIPALS AND PROFESSORS.

New College, Edinburgh.

PRINCIPALS.

1843. Thomas Chalmers, D.D.
1847. William Cunningham, D.D.
1862. Robert S. Candlish, D.D.
1874. Robert Rainy, D.D., till Union.

PROFESSORS.

Thomas Chalmers, D.D., Systematic Theology, 1843-1847.
David Welsh, D.D., Church History, 1843-1845.
William Cunningham, D.D., Apologetics, etc., 1843-1845.
John Duncan, D.D., Hebrew, 1843-1870.

Appendix III

Alexander Black, D.D., Exegetical Theology, 1844-1856.

Patrick M'Dougall, Moral Philosophy, 1844-1852, appointed to the University of Edinburgh, chair not filled up.

William Cunningham, D.D., Church History, 1845-1861.

James Buchanan, D.D., Apologetics, etc., 1845-1847.

John Fleming, D.D., Natural Science, 1845-1857.

Alexander C. Fraser, Logic, 1846-1856, transferred to University, chair not filled up.

James Buchanan, D.D., Systematic Theology, 1847-1868.

Robert S. Candlish, D.D., Apologetics, etc., 1847-1848.

James Bannerman, D.D., Apologetics, etc., 1849-1868.

George Smeaton, D.D., Exegetical Theology, 1857-1889.

Robert Rainy, D.D., Church History, 1862 till Union.

Andrew B. Davidson, D.D., Hebrew, 1863 till Union.

John Duns, D.D., Natural Science, 1864 till Union.

Alexander Duff, D.D., Evangelistic Theology, 1867-1878.

James M'Gregor, D.D., Systematic Theology, 1868-1881.

William G. Blaikie, D.D., Apologetics, etc., 1868-1897.

Thomas Smith, D.D., Evangelistic Theology, 1880-1892.

John Laidlaw, D.D., Systematic Theology, 1881 till Union.

Marcus Dods, D.D., Exegetical Theology, 1889 till Union.

Alexander Martin, D.D., Apologetics, etc., 1897 till Union.

Aberdeen College.

PRINCIPALS.

1864. James Lumsden, D.D.
1876. David Brown, D.D.
1898. Stewart D. F. Salmond, D.D.

PROFESSORS.

Alexander Black, D.D., 1843-1844.

James M'Lagan, D.D., 1846-1852.

Patrick Fairbairn, D.D., 1853-1856.

George Smeaton, D.D., 1854-1857.

Marcus Sachs, Professor of Hebrew, 1855-1869.

James Lumsden, D.D., Systematic Theology, etc., 1856-1875.

David Brown, D.D., Exegetical Theology, etc., 1857-1886.

William Robertson Smith, D.D., Hebrew, 1870-1881.

William Binnie, D.D., Church History, 1875-1886.

Stewart D. F. Salmond, D.D., Systematic Theology, etc., 1876 till Union.

George Cameron, D.D., Hebrew, 1882 till Union.
James Iverach, D.D., Apologetics, etc., 1887 till Union.
James Robertson, D.D., Church History, 1887 till Union.

Glasgow College.

PRINCIPALS.

1857. Patrick Fairbairn, D.D.
1875. George Douglas, D.D.

PROFESSORS.

Patrick Fairbairn, D.D., Divinity, 1856-1874.
James Gibson, D.D., Church History, 1856-1871.
William Hetherington, D.D., Divinity, 1857-1865.
George Douglas, D.D., Hebrew, 1857-1892.
Islay Burns, D.D., Divinity, 1865-1872.
Thomas M. Lindsay, D.D., Church History, 1872 till Union.
James Candlish, D.D., Divinity, 1872-1897.
Alexander B. Bruce, D.D., Apologetics and Exegetics, 1875-1899.
Henry Drummond, Natural Science, 1883-1897.
George Adam Smith, D.D., LL.D., Hebrew, 1892 till Union.
James Denny, D.D., Divinity, 1897 till Union.

Appendix III

UNITED FREE CHURCH OF SCOTLAND.

Moderators since the Union.

*1900. Robert Rainy, D.D., Edinburgh, Principal.
*1901. T. Kennedy, D.D., Edinburgh, North Richmond Street.
*1902. Robert Howie, D.D., Glasgow, St. Mary's, Govan.
*1903. George Robson, D.D., Perth, Bridgend.
 1904. R. G. Balfour, D.D., Edinburgh, New North.
*1905. Robert Rainy, D.D., Edinburgh (second time).

Those marked by asterisks are still living.

Dr. Rainy was previously Moderator of the Free Church Assembly, and Dr. Kennedy, Moderator of the United Presbyterian Synod. Dr. George Hutton, Paisley, Moderator-Elect for 1906, has also been Moderator of the United Presbyterian Synod. The Assembly of 1902 was held in Glasgow, the others in Edinburgh, 1900 in the Waverley Market, 1901, 1903, 1904 in the Assembly Hall on the Mound, 1905 in the Synod Hall, Castle Terrace.

Principal Clerks.

1900. Andrew Melville, D.D., Edinburgh.
1900. Thomas Kennedy, D.D., Edinburgh, retired 1902.
1900. Archibald Henderson, D.D., Crieff.
1900. William Blair, D.D., Dunblane.

Depute Clerk.

1900. Robert S. Simpson, W.S.

Appendix III

PRINCIPALS AND PROFESSORS.

New College, Edinburgh.

PRINCIPAL.

1900. Robert Rainy, D.D.

PROFESSORS.

Robert Rainy, D.D., Church History, 1900-1901.
Andrew B. Davidson, D.D., LL.D., Hebrew, 1900-1902.
John Duns, D.D., Natural Science, 1900-1903.
James A. Paterson, D.D., Hebrew, 1900.
John Laidlaw, D.D., Dogmatics, 1900-1904.
Marcus Dods, D.D., Exegetical Theology, 1900.
James Wardrop, D.D., Dogmatics, 1900-1903.
Alexander Martin, D.D., Apologetics, 1900.
Alexander R. MacEwen, Church History, 1901.
Hugh R. Mackintosh, D.Phil., Dogmatics, 1904.
James Y. Simpson, D.Sc., Natural Science, 1904.

Aberdeen College.

PRINCIPALS.

1900. Stewart D. F. Salmond, D.D., 1900-1905.
1905. James Iverach, D.D.

PROFESSORS.

Robert Johnstone, D.D., Exegetical Theology, 1900.
Stewart D. F. Salmond, D.D., Dogmatics, 1900-1905.

George G. Cameron, D.D., Hebrew, 1900.
James Iverach, D.D., Apologetics, 1900.
James Robertson, D.D., Church History, 1900-1901.
James Stalker, D.D., Church History, 1902.

Glasgow College.

PRINCIPALS.

1900. George C. M. Douglas, D.D., } *Joint*, 1900-1902.
George C. Hutton, D.D.,
1902. Thomas M. Lindsay, D.D.

PROFESSORS.

Thomas M. Lindsay, D.D., Church History, 1900.
James Orr, D.D., Apologetics and Dogmatics, 1900.
Alexander Hislop, D.D., Practical Training, etc., 1900-1906.
George Adam Smith, D.D., LL.D., Hebrew, 1900.
James Denny, D.D., Exegetical Theology, 1900.

Note.—In the above lists we have designated as D.D. those Moderators and Professors who received that degree, though it may not have been bestowed upon them when they were appointed to their respective chairs.

APPENDIX IV.

TABLE OF SOME OF THE EVENTS IN SCOTTISH ECCLESIASTICAL HISTORY.

1560. The Scottish Parliament set aside the Church of Rome as the National Church, and adopted the Confession of Faith known as Knox's Confession.

The first General Assembly of the Presbyterian Church met.

1567. The Presbyterian Church Established by Parliament.

1572. Episcopacy introduced.

1592. Great Charter of the Church passed by Parliament.

1603. James VI. ascended the English Throne.

1637. Introduction of Liturgy of Charles I. Riot in St. Giles.

1638. The National Covenant signed in Greyfriars' Churchyard.

The Glasgow Assembly met. Episcopacy abolished.

Appendix IV

1643.	The Westminster Assembly met.
1647.	The Westminster Confession of Faith adopted by the General Assembly.
1649.	Approval of the Same by the Estates of Parliament.
1660.	The Restoration of Charles II.
1661.	The Restoration of Episcopacy. The Recissory Act.
1662.	The Ejection of upwards of Three Hundred Ministers.
1679.	Battles of Drumclog and Bothwell Bridge.
1680.	The First Sanquhar Declaration.
	Death of Richard Cameron at Airsmoss.
1681.	Formation of the Societies at Logan House, Lesmahagow.
1683-88.	The Ministry of James Renwick.
1685.	The Second Sanquhar Declaration.
1688.	Martyrdom of Renwick.
	The Revolution.
1690.	The Westminster Confession adopted by Parliament.
	The Presbyterian Church Established. General Assembly met.
	The Ministers of the Societies admitted to the Establishment.
1706.	John M'Millan joined the Societies.
1707.	The Union between England and Scotland.
1712.	Restoration of Patronage.
1718-22.	Marrow Controversy.
1732.	Ebenezer Erskine's Synod Sermon.

Appendix IV

1733. The Seceders separated from the Establishment, and formed a Presbytery at Gairney Bridge.
1740. They were deposed by the General Assembly.
1743. Reformed Presbyterian Presbytery formed. The Seceders signed the Covenant.
1745. The Seceders formed a Synod.
1747. The Secession divided into Burghers and Anti-Burghers.
1749. The Inverkeithing Case.
1752. Gillespie deposed by the General Assembly.
1753. M'Millan died.
1754. Ebenezer Erskine died.
1758. Gillespie joined by Thomas Boston, Jun.
1761. Relief Presbytery formed.
1773. Relief Synod formed.
1774. Gillespie died.
1794. Relief Hymn Book issued.
1799. Three Ministers separated from the Burgher Synod and formed the Associate Presbytery.
1805. The Original Associate Synod formed.
1806. Four Ministers separated from the Anti-Burgher Synod and formed the Constitutional Presbytery.
1810. Dr. Andrew Thomson commenced his ministry in Edinburgh. Evangelical Revival.
1811. Reformed Presbyterian Synod formed.
1820. The Breach between the Burghers and Anti-Burghers healed. United Associate Synod formed.

Appendix IV

- 1821. A Secession from that Synod. This united in 1827 with the Constitutional Presbytery and formed the Original Secession Synod.
- 1834. The Veto and Chapel Acts passed by the General Assembly of the Church of Scotland.
- 1838. The Auchterarder Case decided in the Court of Session.
- 1839. The Lethendy Case. The Presbytery of Dunkeld rebuked by the Court of Session.

    The majority of the Original Associate Synod united with the Church of Scotland.
- 1841. Mr. Edwards settled at Marnoch. The seven Strathbogie Ministers deposed by the General Assembly.
- 1842. The Union of the Minority of the Original Associate Synod with the Original Secession Synod.

    The Claim of Right adopted by the General Assembly.

    The Convocation.
- 1843. Decision in the Stewarton Case.

    The Claim of Right rejected by the House of Commons.

    The Protest. The Disruption. The Deed of Demission. The Free Church of 1843.
- 1847. The Secession and Relief formed the United Presbyterian Church.

    Chalmers died.

Appendix IV

1852.	The Union of the Majority of the Original Seceders with the Free Church.
1858.	The Associate Presbytery of Ireland received into the United Presbyterian Church.
1863.	Disruption of the Reformed Presbyterian Synod.
1863-73.	Union Negotiations.
1876.	The English Section of the United Presbyterian Church joined the English Presbyterians.
	The Larger Reformed Presbyterian Synod joined the Free Church.
1879.	United Presbyterian Declaratory Act passed.
1892.	Free Church Declaratory Act passed.
1894.	Formation of the Free Presbyterian Church.
1900.	Union of the Free and United Presbyterian Churches.
	The Free Church of 1900.
1904.	Decision by House of Lords in the Case of Bannatyne *v.* Overtoun.

INDEX OF THE PRINCIPAL NAMES (Persons and Topics).

A

Aberdeen College, 109.
Aberdeen, George, Earl of, 77, 146.
Aberdeen, John, Earl of, 178.
Airsmoss, 14.
Anderson, James, Carluke, 141.
Anderson, William, Loanhead, 156.
Anti-Burghers, 46, 49, 51, 227.
Assembly, General, Church of Scotland, 1638, 6; 1690, 21; 1720, 35; 1722, 36; 1734, 39; 1739, 39; 1740, 40; 1751, 57; 1752, 59; 1753, 59; 1831, 68; 1832, 69; 1834, 70; 1841, 76; 1842, 87; 1843, 92; *seq.*
Assembly, Commission of 1733, 37; 1751, 56; 1838, 72; 1839, 73; 1843, 89, 99.
Assembly, General, of the Free Church, 1843, 99; 1851, 125; 1852, 141; 1853, 147; 1867, 150; 1873, 151; 1876, 159; 1893, 165; 1900, 171; 1905, 190.
Associate Synod, 43, 220.
Atonement, The, 39, 151, 168.
Atonement Controversy, *see* Evangelical Union.
Auchterarder, Case of, 72, 73, 87, 88.
Auld, William, 133.

B

Bannantyne, Colin A., 188, 191, 192.
Begg, Dr. James, Edinburgh, 70, 151, 161.
Bond, Children's, 15, 205.
Boston, Thomas, 35, 55.
Boston, Thomas, Jun., 60.
Boyd, William, 24.
Boyle, Lord President, 193.
Bristo Street, 43, 49, 131.
Brougham, Lord, 119.
Brown, John, of Broughton Place, Edinburgh, 51, 97.
Brown, John, Haddington, 52.
Bryce, Dr. James, 122.
Buchanan, Dr. Robert, 70, 110, 116, 176.
Burgess Oath, 43.
Burghers, The, 43, *seq.* 220.
Bute, Marquis of, 87, 94.

C

Cairns, Principal, 136, 149, 161, 165.
Cameron, Richard, 11-14, 17, 198.
Cameronians, *see* Reformed Presbyterians.
Campbell of Row, 68.
Campbell, Lord, 91.
Campbeltown, Case of, 130, 193.

Index

Candlish, Dr. R. S., 68, 100, 110, 142.
Cardross Case, 148.
Cargil, Donald, 9, 14, 17.
Carstairs, William, 22, 34, 177.
Catechisms, Large and Shorter, 8, 42, 137.
Chalmers, Dr. John, 61.
Chalmers, Dr. Thomas, 65 to 70, 86 to 100, 107, 109, 112, 124, 198, 199.
Chalmers, Dr. Thomas, Death and Funeral of, 113, 114.
Chapel Act, 71, 72, 84, 101.
Charles I., 6.
Charles II., 10, 12, 21.
Churches (Scotland) Act, 1905, 201.
Civil Magistrate, 45, 61.
Claim of Right, 85, *seq.* 89, 95, 125, 146, 182, 189, 192.
Clelland, James, *see* Stewarton Case.
Clelland, William, of Douglas, 23.
Cockburn, Lord, 73, 85.
Colinsburgh, Relief Congregation, 61.
Colier, Thomas, 61.
Colonsay, Lord, 95.
Commons, House of, 89.
Communion, Free, 63, 138.
Confession, *see* Scottish, and Westminster.
Convocation, The, 87, *seq.*
Covenant, National, Solemn League, Covenants, 6, 8, 42, 48, 61, 78, 125, 138, 162, 182, 194.
Craig, Dr. John, 132.
Crawford, William Howeson of Crawfordland, 2.
Crawfordjohn, 26, 27.
Cuming, Dr. Patrick, 57.
Cunningham of Lainsaw, 84.

Cunningham, Principal Wm., 68, 70, 87, 109, 116, 126, 149, 176.

D

Dalziel, William, 106.
Declaratory Acts, 166, 180, 191.
Deed of Demission, 99.
Disestablishment, 166.
Disruption, 96, 103.
Disruption Annals, 108, 114.
Disruption Ministers, 108, *seq.*
Divinity Hall, 164.
Doddridge, Dr., 55.
Duff, Alex., 68, 110, 142, 161.
Dunfermline Presbytery, 36, 57.
Dunlop, Alex. Murray, 85, 142, 148

E

Elder, William, 106.
English Presbyterians, 149.
Episcopacy, Episcopalians, 6, 10, 19, 101.
Erskine, Ebenezer, 31 to 45, 66, 82, 114, 130, 143, 199.
Erskine, Ralph, 31 to 44, 55, 62, 65, 116.
Erskine, John, of Edinburgh, 67.
Evangelical Party, 69.
Evangelical Union, 52.

F

Ferguson, Andrew, Maryton, 107.
Fisher, Edward, 35.
Fisher, James, 38.

Formula of Free Church, 126.
Formula of United Free Church, *see* Uniting Act.
Forrest, Sir James, 95, 100.
Fox Maule, Honourable, 90, 148.
Free Church of 1843, 104, 121, 147, 188, 250.
Free Church of 1900, 182 to 192.
Free Presbyterian Church, 167, 185.
Frew, Dr. Robert, 137, 184, 185, 199.
Fullarton, Lord, 73.

G

Gairney Bridge, 38, 70.
Geddes, Jenny, 6.
Gib, Adam, 43.
Gillespie, Thomas, 54 to 67, 93, 138, 163, 188, 198.
Gladstone, W. E., 98, 147.
Glasgow Assembly, 6, 7.
Glasgow College, 109.
Glenlee, Lord, 73, 84.
Goldie, Dr. John, 37.
Gordon, Dr. Robert, 87.
Goold, Dr. W. H., 155, 160, 162.
Graham, Sir James, 87, 147.
Great Charter of the Church, 6, 20.
Greig, David, 50.
Guthrie, James, 11, 16, 162.
Guthrie, Dr. Thomas, 41, 110.

H

Hamilton, Patrick, 4.
Hanna, Dr., 112.
Henderson, Alexander, 7, 11, 22, 34, 65, 143, 157, 163.
Henderson, Dr. Andrew, 174.
Henderson, John, of Park, 134.
Hill, D. O., 99.
Hillmen, 93, 160, 162.
Hog of Carnock, 35, 55.
Holyrood, Levée at, 1.
Hope, John, 72.
Hutchison, Dr., 166.
Hymn Book, Relief, 63.

I

Inglis, Dr. John, 29, 67, 69.
Innes, Taylor, LL.D., 23.
Inverkeithing, Case of, 56.
Ireland, Associate Presbytery of, 137.
Irish Presbyterian Church, Deputation of, 99.
Ivory, Lord, 84.

J

James IV., 4.
James V., 4.
James VI., 5.
James VII., 10, 18.
Jamieson, Dr. John, 49, 50.
Jedburgh Relief Congregation, 60.
Jeffrey, Lord, 73.
Johns, The Four, 29.
Johns, The Six, 4.
Jubilee, Free Church, 1843, 165.
Jubilee, United Presbyterian Church, 165.

K

Kennedy, Hew, 21.
Kidston, Dr. Wm., 134.
Knox, John, 4, 20, 22, 143.

Index

L

Lambie, Andrew, Pitcairngreen, 140.
Laud, Archbishop, 6.
Lawson, Dr. George, 47, 50.
Lethendy, Case of, 73.
Linning, Thomas, 23.
Logan, George, of Eastwood, 107.
Logan, George, Edinburgh, 39.
Logan House, Lesmahagow, 15.

M

M'Cheyne, 78, 112.
M'Crie, Dr. Charles, 189.
M'Crie, Dr. Thomas, Sen., 48, 49.
M'Crie, Dr. Thomas, Jun., 142.
MacDonald, Donald, of Shieldaig, 169.
Macfarlane, Donald, Raasay, 169.
Macfarlan, Dr. Patrick, 87, 100, 108.
MacKellar, Dr. Angus, 142.
MacKelvie, Dr., 130.
Mackenzie, Roderick, 60.
M'Millan, John, 25, *seq.* 44, 45, 198.
M'Millan, John, Jun., 29.
MacNaughton, Lord, 192.
M'Neil, John, 27.
M'Ward, Robert, 11.
Mair, Dr. Alex., 173 to 177.
Mair, Thomas, of Orwell, 38.
Marnoch, Case of, 74, 75.
Marrow of Modern Divinity, 35, 55.
Mary, Queen, 3.
Meadowbank, Lord, 193.
Medwyn, Lord, 193.
Melbourne, Viscount, 77.
Melville, Andrew, 5, 143.
Miller, Hugh, 119, 120.
Ministers of the Free Church, 1843, 106 to 117.
Ministers withdrawing from the Church, 1662, 9.
Missionary Record, United Free Church, Cover of, 3, 65, 128, 146.
Moderate, Moderates, 57, 67.
Moncreiff, Sir Henry, Sen., 67.
Moncreiff, Sir Henry Wellwood, Jun., 79, 112, 159.
Moncreiff, Lord, 73.
Moncreiff, Lord-Justice Clerk, 78.
Moncrieff, Alex., 38, 39, 40.
Morison, James, 52.
Mutual Eligibility, 151.

N

Nairn of Abbotshall, 27, 38.
Naismith of Dalmeny, 37.
New College, Edinburgh, 109.
Newlands, Dr., 133.
Non-Intrusionists, 70.

O

Oliver, Dr. Alex., 173.
Original Associate Synod, 49, 80, *seq.* 107, 236.
Original Secession Synod, 51, 99, 125, 139, 143, *seq.* 240.

P

Panmure, *see* Fox Maule.

Index

Patronage, 2, 21, 27, 36, 56, 69, 88.
Paxton, Professor George, 48, 51.
Peel, Sir Robert, 1, 77, 90, 98, 147.
Presbytery, Constitutional, 51.
Presbytery, Reformed, 28.
Presbytery, Relief, 61.
Presbytery, Secession, 38, 70.
Protest of the Erskines, 38.
Protest, Free Church, 95.
Protesters, Synod of, 239.

Q

Questions at Ordination, etc., *see* under Formula.

R

Rainy, Principal, 109, 151, 161, 176.
Reformation, The Church of, 3, 4.
Reformed Presbyterians, 29, 59, 121, 124, 125, 155, 216.
Reid, Professor, Glasgow, 26.
Relief Synod, 54, 61, 69, 121, 124, 125, 129, 242.
Renwick, James, 15, 17, 23, 54, 162, 198.
Restoration, 8.
Revolution, Church of, 22, 23, 34.
Revolution Settlement, 2, 18, 24, 26, 42, 46, 64, 70, 78, 127, 144, 163, 182, 190, 201.
Riding Commission, 36, 56.
Right, *see* Claim of.
Robertson, Principal, 56, 67, 85.
Robertson, Lord, 193.
Rutherfurd, Lord, 72, 90.

S

St. Andrew's Church, Edinburgh, 97.
Sanquhar Declarations, 12, 16.
Scot of Gateshaw, 44.
Scottish Confession, 3, 4, 8, 20.
Seceders, Secession, Secession Church, Secession Synod, 25, 28, 31, 39, 40, 42, 43, 61, 69, 121, 124, 125, 128.
Separation, 31, 54, 128.
Separation of Burgher and Anti-Burgher, 46.
Separation in Reformed Presbyterian Synod, 155.
Session, Court of, 72, 74, 75, 84.
Shields, Alexander, 23, 24.
Simson, Professor, 34.
Sinclair, Sir George, 142, 148.
Smith, Dr. Thomas, 79, 108, 152, 184, 195.
Smith, Dr. Walter C., 165.
Society Men and Societies, 14, 17, 24, 160, 163.
Spiritual Independence, 5, 23, 30, 46, 61, 86, 87, 91, 119, 127, 138, 144, 148, 163.
Stanley, Dean, 62.
Stevenson, George, D.D., 51.
Stewarton, Case of, 84.
Stuart, Mary II., 19.
Subordinate Standards, etc., of the Free Church, 125.
Symingtons, 29.
Synod, Reformed Presbyterian, 29, 146, 155, 158.
Synod, United Associate, 50, 51, 52.
Synod, United Presbyterian, 1863, 149; 1873, 151; 1877, 167; 1879, 167; May 1900, 171; Oct. 1900, 171.

Index

T

Tanfield Hall, Canonmills, 97, 131, 142.
Taylor, Dr. Walter Ross of Glasgow, 173, *seq.*
Ten Years' Conflict, 65, 69, 92.
Testimony, Testimonies, 29, 49, 52.
Thomson, Dr. Andrew, 67, 69.
Thomson of Burntisland, 39.
Torphichen Case, 56.

U

Umpherston, Charles, 28.
Union, 31, 128.
Union of Burgher and Anti-Burgher, 50, 233.
Union of Old Light Burghers with Church of Scotland, 77, *seq.*
Union between Old Light Burghers and Old Light Anti-Burghers, 139.
Union of Secession and Relief, 128 to 133, 245.
Union, Original Seceders with Free Church, 139 to 145.
Union, Sir George Sinclair's movement towards, 148.
Union Negotiations, 143 to 151.
Union, United Presbyterian English Synod with English Presbyterians, 154.
Union, Reformed Presbyterians and Free Church, 155 to 161.
Union, Basis of United Presbyterian, 137.
Union, the Free and United Presbyterian, 170 to 176.
Uniting Act, 171, 176, 177.
United Free Church, 17, 45, 155, 170, 258.
United Presbyterian, 135 to 137, 148, 164, 167.
United Presbyterian Church, Synod of, 245.

V

Veto Act, 70, 71, 73, 101.
Voluntary, Voluntaries, 53, 69, 124.

W

Warner, Thomas, Balmoclellan, 107.
Waverley Market, 172.
Welsh, Dr. David, 87, 89, 94, 98, 100, 109, 116.
Westminster Assembly, 8.
Westminster Confession, 8, 20, 42, 55, 63, 92, 126, 137, 159, 166, 178, 179, 190, 192, 201.
White, William, of Haddington, 142, 143.
William III., 2, 19, 24, 93.
Wilson, William, Perth, 38, 41, 42, 143.
Wishart, George, 4.
Witness, Newspaper, 118.
Wood, Dr., Dumfries, 150.
Wright, James, Edinburgh, 140.
Wright, John, of Alloa, 81.

www.ingramcontent.com/pod-product-compliance
Lightning Source LLC
Chambersburg PA
CBHW050342230426
43663CB00010B/1963